The Life You Want Your Kids to Live

Les Parrott III
PARROTT
and Les Parrott Sr.

Beacon Hill Press of Kansas City
Kansas City, Missouri

ISBN 083-411-9021

Printed in the
United States of America

Cover Design: Kevin Williamson

All Scripture quotations not otherwise designated are from the *Holy Bible, New International-al Version*® (NIV®). Copyright © 1973, 1978, 1984 by International Bible Society. Used by permission of Zondervan Publishing House. All rights reserved.

Permission to quote from the following additional copyrighted version of the Bible is acknowledged with appreciation:

New American Standard Bible® (NASB®), © copyright The Lockman Foundation 1960, 1962, 1963, 1968, 1971, 1972, 1973, 1975, 1977, 1995.

Scripture quotation marked KJV is from the King James Version.

Library of Congress Cataloging-in-Publication Data

Parrott, Les.
   The life you want your kids to live / Les Parrott III and Leslie Parrott Sr.
     p. cm.
   ISBN 0-8341-1902-1 (pb.)
    1. Parenting—Religious aspects—Christianity. I. Parrott, Leslie, 1922- II. Title.

BV4529 .P38 2001
248.8'45—dc21

2001025949

10   9   8   7   6   5   4   3   2

Dedicated to
John Leslie Parrott,
the fifth grandchild of
Les Parrott Sr.
and first son of
Les Parrott III

*If you are a parent, recognize that it is the most important
calling and rewarding challenge you have.
What you do every day, what you say and how you act,
will do more to shape the future than any other factor.*
—Marion Wright Edelman

Contents

How to Use This Book

This book is designed to be used in any of a variety of ways. You can read it through alone, making a journal with the study questions at the end of each chapter—adding other thoughts, scriptures, examples, and prayers as they come to your mind.

This is also an excellent tool for parents to study together—whether you're new parents or a seasoned mom and dad. Read the chapters together, talking over the ideas and figuring ways you can apply these words to your family and your children's individual needs. Use the study questions to discover your parenting attitudes, seeing where you're facing the task in the same mind-set and where your ideas vary.

You can also use this book for a small-group study, parents' class, or Sunday School class. You might assign the chapters ahead of time, coming together to discuss them—using the study questions to help get dialogue going. Or, the chapters are short enough to have different members of the group read portions of them aloud during your time together. Through this method, you can support, pray for, and help each other through the challenges and joys of parenting.

No matter what way you use this book, we hope it will help you teach your kids to successfully lead *the life you want your kids to live.*

About the Authors

DR. LES PARROTT III is founder and codirector (with his wife, Dr. Leslie Parrott) of the Center for Relationship Development on the campus of Seattle Pacific University, a groundbreaking program dedicated to teaching the basics of good relationships. He is a professor of psychology at Seattle Pacific University as well as the author of several best-selling books, including the award-winning *Saving Your Marriage Before It Starts, Becoming Soul Mates,* and *When Bad Things Happen to Good Marriages.* He has written for a variety of magazines, and his work has been featured in *USA Today* and the *New York Times.* He has appeared on CNN, *Good Morning America,* and *Oprah.* More information and resources are available at <www.realrelationships.com>.

DR. LESLIE PARROTT SR. is pastor in residence at the Biltmore Church of the Nazarene in Phoenix. He served as college president for 22 years at Eastern Nazarene College (ENC) and Olivet Nazarene University (ONU). Major pastorates have included ministry at Flint, Michigan; Portland, Oregon; and Puyallup, Washington. Dr. Parrott also served as chairman of the psychology department at George Fox College. He is the author of two dozen books and is a graduate of Olivet Nazarene College (now ONU) with an M.A. from Willamette University and an earned Ph.D. from Michigan State University.

Introduction

"When you were a young parent," I asked my dad over lunch in downtown Seattle, "did you ever think about the qualities you wanted your kids to have?"

He thought for a moment and said, "Sure—I had some things in mind."

"Like what?" I asked.

"Well, your mother and I did our best to make sure each of you boys grew up in a home where you would find a relationship with God."

"OK, but that's kind of a given," I pressed. "You were a pastor!"

"Well, that's true," Dad confessed. "But there were other things."

"What were they?" I asked again.

Dad put down his fork and sipped his coffee. "You're serious about this, aren't you?"

I nodded my answer as I ate another bite of my sandwich.

"Let me think," he started.

That thinking lasted far longer than I could have ever anticipated. As Dad started to tell me about some of the character qualities he and Mom tried to impart to us kids, I borrowed a pen from the waiter and began taking notes. It's a habit I picked up—well—from Dad. Besides, as a psychologist, I thought this information could give me a glimpse into what my former professors called "transgenerational inheritance"—psychobabble for the life lessons you learn from your parents.

Dad and I eventually moved our conversation to the lobby of a nearby hotel. That's where I began to see what was going on deep down in the mind of the man I called Dad. That's where I learned for the first time what kind of character he had tried to carve into my two older brothers and me. And that's where I decided I would be intentional about the qualities I would teach to my children.

At that time, my wife and I had given birth to a couple of doctoral degrees, but no children. A year later, however, our son John was born. And in the year after his birth I reviewed the notes from that daylong conversation with Dad. Around that time, an editor from Beacon Hill Press of Kansas City called to ask if I had ever considered writing a book with my father. I took it as a sign and phoned Dad. We began organizing my notes from our conversation and formulating the book you now hold.

This includes some of the most personal writing either of us has ever done. Of the dozen or so books I've written, and the more than 20 Dad has authored, neither of us has ever been more compelled to examine the qualities we prize most deeply.

Here you will find the nine characteristics or virtues we believe comprise a life well lived. Here you will find the nine teachable traits Mom and Dad have tried to pass on to me, and the same nine traits my wife and I will try to pass on to our children. We offer these traits not necessarily as the definitive list every parent should ascribe to. But we believe, after much self-examination and research, that these qualities leave a lasting legacy—one that sets children on the road less traveled. We believe they make all the difference in the success, and in the spiritual and emotional well-being, of a person's life—from generation to generation.

—*Les Parrott III*

Let me clarify something. Our family includes many people named *Leslie*. The *L* in my father's name, *A. L.* Parrott, stands for *Leslie*. I am *Leslie*. Our oldest son is Richard *Leslie*, and he has a son named Andrew *Leslie*.

When our third son was two years old, we changed his name to *Leslie* to keep the legacy alive. Then he married a lovely young woman named *Leslie*. And when their baby was born, they named him John *Leslie*.

We also have our share of doctorates—Ph.D.'s, Ed.D.'s, D.D.'s, one M.D., and one doctor of letters. Les III, my coauthor, is one of those with both the name and the degree.

I clearly remember the lunch that day in Seattle when Les III asked me about the legacy of traits that my wife, Lora Lee, and I worked to pass on to our kids. The conversation became so animated and long that it's hard to forget. I told Les that as we raised him and his brothers, his mother and I wanted them to grow up loving the church and its leadership. I explained that was why we had so many church leaders to our home for dinner when it would have been far easier for me to take our guests out to a restaurant. I told him this was why we held church board meetings in the parsonage while our children were growing up. I remember our boys pulling their red wagon around the room, serving refreshments to the board.

I reminded Les of the time he and his brothers presented their own proposal to the church board, asking that a basketball hoop be placed over the garage door of the parsonage. The board discussed this proposal and passed it unanimously.

I told Les about the value we placed on family discussions around the dinner table. We didn't even come close to having meals together every night as a family, but we did make this family gathering a priority every Monday evening—complete with a white linen tablecloth and our best silver. Our kids called it "company dinner," whether we invited company or not. During these dinners, we discussed important family issues and whatever else we needed to talk about—including character qualities that would help our kids live the successful lives we hoped they would live.

That day in Seattle Les and I talked about other important qualities his mother and I tried to leave as our legacy to and in our children. Then we began discussing the educational and career goals Lora Lee and I had tried to help our sons discover—being sensitive to their unique personalities and individual interests.

Les reminded me of the time I flew from Chicago to Los Angeles just for a day to help him tackle the challenge of developing his doctoral dissertation. By the end of that day, he had replaced his jitters with a sheaf of notes on yellow pads—which he converted into a successful proposal for his doctoral committee at Fuller Theological Seminary.

Before Les III and I left our discussion that afternoon in Seattle, the idea for this book on the legacy of family virtues and values was born, and I didn't even know it. Only after Les called me with the idea did I begin to see how our conversation might help other parents, especially those just beginning their families. These parents have the potential to shape the character of a young life most dramatically.

In much the same way that parents pass on a name to a child, they also pass along qualities and life lessons that guide that child's path. The table of contents in this book reflects our list of qualities and life lessons. These are the values and virtues I feel my parents, A. L. and Lucille Parrott, left in their family legacy. And these are the traits we, Leslie and Lora Lee Parrott, have tried to pass on to our three boys and their children.

As you read through these chapters, I hope our list, at least in part, becomes your list as you add to it, delete from it, personalize it, and make it your own.

—Leslie Parrott Sr.

THINK WELL
OF YOURSELF

If I am not for myself, who is for me?
And if I am only for myself, what am I?
—Hillel

I was spending a sweltering August afternoon in Columbus, Ohio, when a physician friend from the Ohio State University Medical Center handed me (Les Sr.) a nondescript paperback book.

"You'll love this," he insisted. "But I want it back."

Before I could do more than flip the pages with my thumb, he was gone. That afternoon, more than three decades ago, I started reading Hugh Missildine's *Your Inner Child of the Past*. And that afternoon became a defining moment for me as a parent. There in Columbus, sitting on a park bench reading this book, I realized just how powerful my imprint on my children's lives would be.

As I read, I learned that Dr. Missildine, then dean of the School of Psychiatry at Ohio State University, had found the traditional Freudian approach of therapy too slow and expensive, especially for the boys and girls he treated at his downtown clinic. Over the years he looked for a more efficient, more dependable, and simpler therapeutic approach to practice with children. His findings as reported in this book opened my eyes to a powerful and fundamental truth about children—a truth we often take for granted these days.

At birth, Dr. Missildine illustrated, it's as though every child is given a piece of unexposed film to be developed in his or her mind. While the child is growing up, a variety of good and bad experiences contribute to the image he or she eventually puts on this film. And that image eventually becomes a self-portrait. When the image on that film in the child's mind is completed, the child's mind says, "This is the kind of person I am."

Like the myriad of tiny dots that eventually become a photo on a piece of paper, every child develops an identity comprised from countless thoughts, feelings, and experiences.

Acceptance of one's intrinsic worth is the core of the personality. When it collapses, everything else begins to quiver.
—James Dobson

A child's experiences with Mom and Dad, of course, play the biggest role in developing this self-evaluation. Everything about the relationship goes into the picture: how the child is hugged or not hugged, encouraged or discouraged; whether Mom smiles or scowls; or whether Dad shows up at a school play or not. All this shapes the child's identity. No incident is too small to be recorded and entered into the self-portrait of a child's mind. The child decides, *I'm smart. I'm dumb. I almost always succeed. I usually fail. I'm quick. I'm slow. I'm good-looking. I'm ugly.*

By the time children are in high school, their self-image is taking full form and becoming a mind-set that will probably last a lifetime. When they reach adulthood, the "inner child of their past" serves as a rudder, steering them in the direction their self-image takes them.

It doesn't matter that the self-image may be inaccurate or distorted. This self-image still directs our most important decisions. It still guides our steps. And because of this, when we consider the lives we want our children to live, we must ensure that they think well of themselves.

What "Thinking Well of Yourself" Means

Dr. Missildine's book may have been the epicenter for a social earthquake he never meant to start. In the years since its publication, traditional views of child-rearing and teaching have been jolted from their foundation. A national movement emerged with one overarching purpose: to boost children's self-esteem. This movement took on an unwieldy life of its own.

Self-esteem, or more accurately the lack of it, quickly became *the* hook on which to hang our children's problems. It was seen as the cause for nearly every social problem of youth. Because of this movement, everything from low grades to juvenile delinquency was blamed on low self-esteem. Teachers, counselors, and parents from coast to coast began singing the praises of this new movement.

The Massachusetts Soccer Association took the goal of developing children's self-esteem to new heights. No tournament games involving children younger than 10 had winners or losers. And all children on all teams received trophies. As a result, no child ever experienced "the agony of defeat."

Nor did any child experience the true triumph of victory.

This attitude was also reflected in the classroom, where teachers tended to pass children from one grade to the next whether or not they were ready. After all, they reasoned, holding a child back might damage his or her fragile self-esteem.

At the height of this craze, a teacher in Columbia, Missouri, chose one child each day to stand on a table while the others applauded. This was supposed to make the boy or girl feel good for the moment. Research, not surprisingly, failed to back up any long-term, positive effects from false applause or any other superficial strategies. Despite their good intentions, teachers, coaches, counselors, and parents had missed the point.

We cannot manufacture positive self-esteem en masse. It cannot be doled out like trophies. The capacity for children to think well of themselves is instilled over time, deep in the hearts of these little souls. This trait is carefully cultivated by moms and dads who invest in each young person's life to help him or her become a man or woman who possesses dignity and self-respect.

◇ ◇ ◇

Your little ones are a blank tape, constantly running and recording information. Whose information do you want on that tape? Yours or somebody else's?

—Tim Hulett

◇ ◇ ◇

We should not confuse thinking well of ourselves with pride or arrogance. Actually, the attitude of thinking well of ourselves is the opposite of pride. Pride is based on self-doubt. Humility is based on self-worth. A person who thinks well of himself or herself accepts both strengths and weaknesses, while a person filled with pride denies his or her faults.

People who think well of themselves do not practice false humility, which is based on self-deprecation and rejects strengths altogether. People who think well of themselves embrace a humble heart with an accurate self-appraisal and a healthy outlook. They are open to receive both positive and negative feedback.

The practice of thinking well of ourselves develops early in childhood and usually continues unabated for a lifetime. The deep roots of negative self-esteem, on the other hand, are almost impossible to eradicate. Because of this, everyone who invests in a young person's life must consider practical ways to instill this quality.

Before we do this, however, we explore just why this quality is so important when it comes to the lives we want our kids to live.

Why It Matters

A child who never learns to think well of himself or herself becomes an adult who suffers from inferiority. Inferiority can lead to serious problems, such as depression, drug abuse, anxiety disorders, compulsive overeating, broken relationships, and much more. In general, people who feel inferior have few aspirations for success. These people become distractible, shy, withdrawn, inhibited, anxious, or obnoxious adults. No one who cares about the welfare of any child would choose this path for the child he or she loves.

For this reason alone, teaching children to think well of themselves matters. But we also have a biblical call to help children on this journey. And the Bible also shows us plenty of solid examples of this.

*Helping your child toward self-esteem
is the most important gift that
any parent can bestow.*
—T. Berry Brazelton

In the Old Testament, for example, when Joseph was a teenager, he bragged to his brothers about his dreams that they would eventually pay reverence to him by bowing to him. As a result of Joseph's arrogance and his brothers' jealousy of him, his brothers eventually sold him into slavery (Gen. 37).

After his brothers' betrayal, Joseph spent 13 years living in slavery in Egypt, far away from his homeland of Canaan—and he was also thrown into prison on false charges. When he was just 30 years old, his God-given dreams of plenty and famine led him to be appointed as one of the most powerful men in Egypt. When his brothers traveled to Egypt looking for food, they encountered him again, and his brothers did indeed bow to him—40 years after selling him into slavery.

Joseph took his family into his household during the bad years and beyond. Seventeen years after coming to Egypt to live with his sons, Jacob died. Joseph's brothers were sure that, without their father to intercede for them, Joseph would finally rain vengeance on them for their mistreatment of him 40 years earlier.

Instead, he said, "'You meant evil against me, but God meant it for good. . . . [Fear not.] I will provide for you and your little ones.' So he comforted them and spoke kindly to them" (Gen. 50:20-21, NASB).

A person who does not think well of himself would never do this. That's one reason this quality is so important. Self-dignity enables kindness.

The New Testament shows us this trait in Paul's life. Paul was terribly mistreated in Philippi. He had endured a miscarriage of justice and faced the memories of his agony beneath whiplashes and the stocks of a vermin-infested cell. In this setting, Paul wrote to his dear friend and former intern, Timothy, an admonition about thinking well of yourself: "Do your best to present yourself to God as one approved, a workman who does not need to be ashamed and who correctly handles the word of truth" (2 Tim. 2:15).

The Bible often refers to us as God's "children" (1 John 5:1-2). God does not want His children feeling bad about themselves. God loves His children (John 3:16). There is "no condemnation" (Rom. 8:1-2) for His children. The bottom line? As Christians, we have good reason to think well of ourselves. We have worth because God created us and because Christ died for our sins.

How to Instill Self-Worth in a Child

If you could gather child development experts from around the world and ask them how to cultivate a healthy sense of self-worth in a child, you would be bombarded by innumerable tips and techniques. The possibilities to provide a little ego boost are endless. But here are a few of the most effective methods for going below the surface to where it really matters, where this quality will abide.

You may find some points more helpful than others, but all

can be woven into the fabric of your specific situation as you consider your child's individual needs. Whether you are a teacher, a counselor, a coach, a pastor, a parent, or anyone else involved in a youngster's life, we offer these with a prayer that they will help you as you help children mold a positive internal self-image that will last for their whole lives.

◇ ◇ ◇

Self-esteem is the reputation we acquire with ourselves.
—Nathaniel Branden

◇ ◇ ◇

Underscore God's love. Leslie and I (Les III) had just stepped onto the platform in the Rose Garden Arena in Portland, Oregon, where nearly 15,000 people had assembled for a mega marriage seminar. That night, the six speakers were to briefly outline what they would discuss during the workshops they taught. Just before Leslie and I stepped to the podium, our friend Gary Smalley captivated the crowd by holding up a crisp $50 bill and asking the massive audience, "Who would like this $50 bill?"

We saw hands wave everywhere. Gary said, "I will give this $50 to one of you, but first let me do this." He crumpled up the bill and then asked, "Who still wants it?" The same hands went up in the air.

"Well," he replied, "what if I do this?" He dropped it on the ground and ground it with his shoe. He picked up the limp money. "Now who still wants it?" Again, hands filled the air.

"You have all learned a valuable lesson," Gary said. "No matter what I did to the money, you still wanted it because it did not decrease in value. It was still worth $50. Many times in our lives we are dropped, crumpled, and ground into the dirt by the decisions we make and the circumstances we face. We feel we are worthless. But no matter what has happened or what will happen, you will never lose your value in God's eyes. Dirty or clean, crumpled or finely creased, you are priceless to Him."

Every child who learns to think well of himself or herself eventually hears the same lesson that crowd in Portland learned. God's love does not depend on how we look or what we do. Every child who understands this biblical truth has a head start in the self-worth game. Why? Because God's love is the very bedrock of thinking well of yourself. When we realize we are members of God's creation, we see we are objects of divine love.

Dignity is not negotiable.
Dignity is the honor of the family.
—Vartan Gregorian

Prize their presence. I (Les Sr.) always did my best to practice this important principle for our boys. As a pastor and later as a college president, my life was often very busy. I could have easily blamed the demands of my work for not letting me spend enough time with my children. I determined not to do that. And though I often failed, each of my boys tells me the individual time we spent together was instrumental in helping them build a positive self-image. When we prize our children's presence, they make a predictable interpretation: Dad thought being with me was more important than being at one of his meetings, so I must be a valuable person.

A friend of ours realized he wasn't spending as much time with his two young girls as he wanted to. After apologizing to them, he said, "You know, the *quality* of time we share is more important than the *quantity* of time we spend together."

The girls, aged 6 and 4, didn't quite understand. Their dad explained, "Quantity means how much time, and quality means how good the time is that we spend together. Which would you rather have?"

The six-year-old replied, "Quality time—and lots of it!"

Every child feels the same way. Quality time has been oversold. Kids who spend more time with their parents feel better about themselves. This is true for toddlers and teens. When teenagers have a problem, they want to talk about it when they're thinking about it. It won't wait until 6:00, when Mom or Dad gets home. The time we set aside to spend with our children sends a powerful message to them that they are valued, that their presence matters to us. If you want to increase a child's odds of thinking well of himself or herself, carve out some space in your time-starved schedule that is routinely dedicated solely to him or her.

Look beyond the bad to find the good. Artist Benjamin West tells how he loved to paint as a youngster. When his mother left the house, he would pull out the oils and try to paint. One day he took out all the paints and made quite a mess. He hoped to get it all cleaned before his mother returned. But she discovered what he had done. West said her response completely surprised him. She picked up his painting and said, "My—what a beautiful painting of your sister!" She gave him a kiss on the cheek and walked away. With that kiss, West says, he became a painter.

What a powerful message! And what an insightful mother! She understood the merit of looking beyond something bad to focus on something good. How easy it would have been for her to focus on her son's mess! Instead, she set that aside to value the good he had done. That simple act helped her son think well of himself and helped him create a self-image that allowed him to discover his calling. That is the power of looking beyond the bad to find the good.

Every day, we parents make messes. We say or do things we later wish we hadn't. Unfortunately, this is part of being human. And the last thing we need is for someone to come along and say, "What a mess you've made!"

Instead, we need a kiss of encouragement. And if we adults long for and need that kind of support and love, just think of how much our children crave it.

Discover their competence. If you're to ever help children think well of themselves, you must understand the connection between self-esteem and basic competence. Self-esteem alone is not enough. We're mistaken to believe that helping our children "feel good" about themselves will foster high achievement. This is only half of the equation for finding enduring success.

The other equally important half is *doing well.* When parents, teachers, and coaches applaud kids who haven't done things that merit praise, this doesn't help them. It's impossible for a child to feel good without first learning to do well. In the long run, only children who learn through experience that they really can handle the tasks of everyday life will possess true confidence in themselves.

"Self-esteem is not the cause of competence," says Martin Ford of George Mason University. "Rather, it's the result of being competent."

So we parents must explore our children's competencies and help them master varied tasks. Find out what your children do well, and celebrate those things. Maybe they're good at building tall towers out of blocks, or maybe they have a terrific sense of direction or can balance well on a beam. Maybe they read at an advanced level or can solve puzzles quickly. Whatever big or little thing they can successfully do is a potential source for helping them think well of themselves.

So don't get the cart before the horse. Praise and applaud areas in which the child is really good. Watch for those especially challenging activities they achieve and master on their own—whether it's pulling off their socks, feeding the cat, or ironing a shirt to wear to school the next morning. The more you praise genuine achievements, the more your children will experience genuinely good feelings about themselves.

DISCUSSION QUESTIONS FOR GROUP STUDY

◆ Do you agree "thinking well of yourself" is an important character quality to pass along to a child? Why or why not?

◆ In what ways have you already tried to help your own child paint a positive self-portrait? What specific statements or actions have you found consistently helpful in building your children's self-worth?

◆ When you think of "your inner child of the past," what emotions stir within you? How do the experiences you had as a child influence your ability to help your child think well of himself or herself?

◆ How did you come to realize your worth in God's eyes? How can you help your child discover his or her worth in God's eyes?

◆ Name at least one specific idea you can try in the next few days to put principles from this chapter into practice.

◆ If your children are toddlers or beyond, jot a quick list of things you can praise them for this week.

Adjust to Things Beyond Your Control

◇ ◇ ◇

You have to accept whatever comes,
and the only important thing is that you meet it
with courage and with the best you have to give.
—Eleanor Roosevelt

In the early 1830s a train of Conestoga wagons rolled through the Cumberland Gap from Virginia into Kentucky. They turned south along the Cumberland Plateau into Tennessee and planned to turn west at Monterey to Nashville. From there, they would go west to Texas.

A young widow with several children drove one of the wagons in the train. After her husband died, her brother in east Texas had sent word that he would help her raise the children if she could just get them to Texas.

The wagon train stopped for the night in a valley just north of Monterey, Tennessee, a few miles from the Kentucky border. A friendly farmer let the widow and her boys spend the night in the haymow of his barn. But the next morning, one of the little boys had the measles.

The wagon master, trying to do his job, told the mother she

had two options: she could stay with the boy, or she could leave him—but he announced that no sick boy could go with the wagon train, for he would surely infect the other pioneers. The widow knew that if she stayed, another wagon train they could join might not come along for months and months. After intense agonizing, the widow decided to leave the little boy with the farmer, promising to return for him as soon as she got her other little ones settled in Texas. But she never came back. Some speculate that she died. Others believe she could not manage the trip back to Tennessee. We'll probably never know why the mother didn't return for her son.

That little boy was my (Les Sr.'s) great-grandfather. And he has left an invaluable legacy to our family.

If you don't like something, change it.
If you can't change it, change your attitude.
Don't complain.
—Maya Angelou

◇ ◇ ◇

Great-Grandfather fought in the Confederacy during the Civil War. His leg was shot off in battle. When the army released him at Murfreesboro, he had to hobble the last 65 miles home on a pair of crutches. What a tortuous journey!

Our family letters from that time, plus all the other bits of information I have gleaned, have revealed that he was a religious man known for loving his family—especially his two boys. One of those sons was my grandfather. I read one of the letters Great-Grandfather wrote from an army hospital where they cut off his leg without giving him the benefit of anesthesia. That upbeat letter to his wife, now in the State Library Archives of Tennessee, told her to hug their two little boys for him and to let them know he'd be coming home. Three years after he returned home, he died.

James Parrott left a legacy that has been handed from generation to generation in our family. This inheritance has nothing to do with money but has everything to do with attitude. Jim, as the family called him, knew the value of adjusting to circumstances beyond his control, and he did his best to pass this quality to his sons. After all, they saw him live the attitudes he encouraged. Jim had every reason to complain and blame others because he grew up without a mom or dad. He could have justifiably grumbled about the results of the war on his life.

Instead, he rose above his challenges. He was known for having an adjustable attitude that softened the jolts he encountered. My father learned this character quality from his father, and I have learned it from my father. This is a quality I have long prized and have tried to pass along to my three sons.

◇ ◇ ◇

The last of the human freedoms is to choose one's attitudes.
—Viktor Frankl

◇ ◇ ◇

We encourage you to pass along this character quality, this capacity to adjust to things beyond your control, to your children. This is an essential ingredient—perhaps one of the main ingredients—for helping our kids experience the lives we want them to live.

What "Adjusting to Situations Beyond Your Control" Means

"The longer I live, the more I realize the impact of attitude on life," writes pastor Chuck Swindoll in his 1981 book *Improving Your Serve.* "Attitude, to me, is more important than facts. It is more important than the past, than education, than money, than circumstances, than failures, than successes, than what other people think or say or do. It is more important than appearance, giftedness, or skill."

Swindoll adds that the most remarkable fact about life is that we can choose our attitude every day of the year. Adjusting to things beyond our control means the ability to take full responsibility for our attitude and be happy in spite of our circumstances.

Attitudes can make or break a person's life. And a positive attitude depends on a person's ability to adjust to situations beyond his or her control. No matter what advantages or disadvantages a person faces, he or she can improve a situation. If we can adjust to circumstances beyond our control, we can reframe a situation and see it in positive terms, rather than in a negative light. This quality also enables us to give others the benefit of the doubt. It lets us set aside blame, resentment, and anger.

***What is the difference between an obstacle
and an opportunity? Our attitude toward
it. Every opportunity has a difficulty, and
every difficulty has an opportunity.***
—J. Sidlow Baxter

◇ ◇ ◇

Each year millions of people are robbed of happiness because they succumb to a negative mind-set, blaming their unhappiness on people and things. Children, as well as adults, say phrases like "He makes me so angry." People can do or say things that tempt us to respond negatively and be upset, but we can choose to take the high road. Being emotionally upset is a natural reaction to something we dislike, but that reaction can trigger a more constructive, positive response. Perhaps this is what the apostle Paul meant when he wrote in Phil. 4:8, "Whatever is true, whatever is noble, whatever is right, whatever is pure, whatever is lovely, whatever is admirable—if anything is excellent or praiseworthy—think about such things."

The ability to adjust when life is beyond our control is the ability to recognize that we, not our circumstances, control our attitudes.

Why Adjusting to Things Beyond Your Control Matters

Some people live radiant, happy, and productive lives. Others who attend the same church listen to the same sermons and sing the same songs as these radiant folks, but they are beaten down, defeated, and riddled with worry. It's no accident that some people can absorb life's jolts, internalize injustice, and then rise above the seemingly unbearable stress of life and be happy anyway.

The reason for the discrepancy is not luck. Nor is it an ability to solve problems—as important as that is. Attitude is the reason some people make the most of their lives while others barely make it at all.

◇ ◇ ◇

I am convinced that life is 10 percent what happens to me and 90 percent how I react to it.
—Chuck Swindoll

◇ ◇ ◇

Once an old dog fell into a farmer's well. After assessing the situation, the farmer sympathized with the dog but decided that neither the dog nor the well were worth the trouble of saving. Instead, he planned to bury the old dog in the well and put him out of his misery.

When the farmer began shoveling dirt into the well, the old dog was hysterical. But as the farmer continued shoveling and the dirt hit his back, the dog started shaking it off and stepping on top of that dirt, blow after blow.

No matter how painful the clods of dirt landing on him were or how distressing the situation seemed, the old dog fought panic and kept shaking off the dirt and stepping up. Before too long, battered and exhausted, he stepped triumphantly over the wall of that well. What seemed as if it would bury him actually benefited him, even saved him—because of the way he handled his adversity.

If we face our problems and respond to them positively—refusing to give in to panic, bitterness, or self-pity—the adversities that come to bury us can potentially bless us if we cultivate the capacity to adjust to situations beyond our control.

How to Instill This Quality in a Child

I have yet to find a best-selling parenting book that includes a chapter on how to cultivate children's capacity to adjust to things beyond their control. Maybe it's because this quality is assumed to be a trait that automatically builds in a person's life as he or she matures. Perhaps it's considered beyond a child's grasp.

> *You are only one thought away*
> *from a good feeling.*
> —Sheila Krystal

However, children are never too young to begin learning about how to be flexible and cope when life throws curveballs. While we must certainly give plenty of grace for a child's emotional impulses, we can quietly cultivate the quality as our children grow up with a few suggestions like these.

Inspire them with examples. I (Les III) will never forget hearing Dad talk about Viktor Frankl, who survived a Nazi concentration camp during World War II. In spite of unspeakable mistreatment by Adolf Hitler's Gestapo, Frankl lived a positive life amid the squalor and death of imprisonment. In his 1984 book *Man's Search for Meaning,* he made a statement that has stuck with me to this day: "We who lived in concentration camps can remember the men who walked through the huts comforting others, giving away their last piece of bread. They may have been few in number, but they offer sufficient proof that everything can be taken from a man but one thing: the last of human freedoms—to choose one's attitude in any given set of circumstances—to choose one's own way."

Viktor Frankl's example still inspires me. And any dramatic or memorable story of a person who has a positive attitude despite his or her circumstances will probably stick in your child's mind. Sharing these inspirational stories with your children is a key to cultivating this quality.

You can find these stories in many different kinds of books. Biographies are a great place to get the stories. Most famous people had to overcome a number of adversities at some point in their lives, whether they're sports heroes or corporate executives. Books about the growth and development of churches, mission outreaches, and ministry organizations are often rife with inspiring stories—so check out those missionary books! Books by motivational speakers and Christian leaders often use inspiring stories as illustrations. And you can even find books filled with short anecdotes, including those about people who have overcome the odds.

Also keep your eyes and ears open as you read magazines and watch television and listen to sermons. Remember those inspiring stories to share with your kids at dinner or other appropriate times—or even write them down and give them to your children (or slip them into a lunch or homework folder, or tape them on your children's bathroom mirror). Let them see how real people overcome real problems, and remind them that God will help them adjust and overcome too.

Disbar discouragement. Perhaps you've heard the story about the devil having a yard sale. All his used tools were spread out and marked with different prices. He offered a fiendish selection. Hatred, jealously, deceit, lying, pride—all of these were expensive. But a tool on display at the side of the yard was more obviously worn than any other tools. Surprisingly, it was also the most costly. It was labeled "discouragement."

When questioned about its high price, the devil said, "It's more useful to me than any other tool. When I can't bring down my victims with any of the other tools, I use discouragement, because so few people realize it belongs to me."

A little discouragement is human and normal, especially for children. But that doesn't mean we should ever wallow in it. Don't let your child stay discouraged too long. When it sets in, the devil can get a foothold in your child's life, for discouragement can lead to doubting God's love and provision.

I have learned the secret of being content in any and every situation, whether well fed or hungry, whether living in plenty or in want.
—the apostle Paul (Phil. 4:12)

◇ ◇ ◇

When you see that your children are discouraged, do what you can to lift their spirits. Eventually, they'll learn to give themselves a pep talk and to talk to God about their stress. Then they will be well on their way overcoming discouragement and adjusting to life situations beyond their control.

Master an even emotional tone. When your car careens into the driveway, and you start up the back steps with a bag of groceries in each arm, how do the children in your house react. Do they say, "Oh, good! Mom's home! Everything will be OK now"?

Or do they freeze in place and wait to see what's going to happen next. "Oh, oh—Mom's back."

When you slam the car door behind you and the kids can hear your heavy steps on the porch, do they squeal with delight, or do they enter an in-between mode, waiting to see what Dad's mood will be like?

Your answer to these questions determines the degree to which your kids have a chance of cultivating the capacity to adjust to things beyond their control. You see, how you manage your emotions speaks volumes to your children about how they can—or can't—do the same thing. The more consistent and stable your emotions, the more likely that your children will follow suit.

◇ ◇ ◇

People are just about as happy as they make up their minds to be.
—Abraham Lincoln

◇ ◇ ◇

Talk to your kids about how misfortune can become good fortune. Earlier we mentioned Joseph, who was sold by his brothers into slavery when he was just a young man. When their father died, the brothers were afraid that Joseph would finally take his revenge on them, although he had been taking care of them for quite a while. They approached Joseph with the most influential lie they could think of: "Before he died, Dad left a message that he wanted you to forgive us for treating you so badly." Joseph saw right through their lie to their fears. In his response to his brothers, Joseph revealed his life philosophy: "You intended to harm me, but God intended it for good to accomplish what is now being done, the saving of many lives" (Gen. 50:20).

Although his brothers' actions led to his slavery and later imprisonment, Joseph didn't see the individual circumstances as tragedies. Instead, he saw the big picture of God's using circumstances to guide him.

God uses unexpected means to get us where He wants us in life. Sometimes God's routes aren't what we would choose, but He uses life's circumstances to teach us and mold us. Look in your own life. Have you ever experienced situations that you were sure were going to destroy your life—but then you saw God use that tragedy or trauma in miraculous ways? Tell these stories to your children. And teach them that God will do the same in their lives.

DISCUSSION QUESTIONS FOR GROUP STUDY

◆ Recall a time when life pitched you a curveball. What did you do?

◆ Do you ever recall your parents facing an unexpected bad circumstance when you were a child? How did they deal with it? What did you learn from the situation?

◆ Sometimes our ability to handle twists and turns in life can reflect our personalities. Which kind of person are you? One who invites changes and challenges, or one who prefers security?

◆ Which of your children are more likely to weather life's changes well? Why?

◆ How can you keep the lines of communication with your children open while they're encountering changes and challenges in life?

3

DELAY YOUR GRATIFICATION

◇ ◇ ◇

Without discipline, there's no life at all.
—Katharine Hepburn

I (Les Sr.) was six years old when I received my first lesson in delayed gratification. That was the year Santa Claus brought me a beautiful new coaster wagon, resplendent with varnished sideboards and red wheels. And that was when my father suggested that I sell my old wagon, a smaller, slightly rusted metal version. I did. Then I had two dollars burning a hole in my pocket.

My father then suggested we go to the bank. That's where, at age six, I received my first savings passbook. I was almost as proud of a savings account opened in my own name as I was of the new wagon. I didn't understand what Dad meant with such words as "interest" and "deposits," but that started me on a savings plan that taught me the value of delayed gratification.

The payoff for this education came when I entered my junior year of college and bought a brand-new car, a tan Plymouth coupe—with cash. By the time Lora Lee and I were married, I had saved enough to furnish a modest apartment with new appliances and furniture. And during that era, we adopted a financial principle that has guided our finances ever since. All of our spending, except for our house, has been based on cash available. If we don't have the cash for it, we don't purchase it.

This principle of delayed gratification enables us to live debt free. But more important, delayed gratification makes a successful life possible. Delayed gratification helps students make good grades in school, makes possible sexual purity in adolescence, and results in worthy careers as young adults. Above all, it enables us to steer clear of sin and honor Christ. It helps us live the fulfilled life God calls each of us to. And in the end, because of delayed gratification, God will say to His servants, "Well done."

Without developing the ability to delay gratification, our children miss one of the important building blocks for a family legacy.

What "Delayed Gratification" Means

Anyone who has ever eaten the crusts of a peanut butter and jelly sandwich *first*—to then enjoy the rest of the sandwich without the cumbersome crusts—knows the meaning of delayed gratification. This occurs anytime a person intentionally endures something less pleasant—no matter how big or how small—to enjoy something better at a later time. Delayed gratification happens when we pay now to play later.

Self-control is at the heart of this quality. Because of that, this is a quality that can be taught. Meir Statman, a finance professor at Santa Clara University in California, says that we all have the capacity to learn self-control, just as we can learn a different language. When parents teach their children that they have to wait for something they want, he says, their children learn a valuable lesson.

And that valuable lesson is delayed gratification.

When I was a child, Mom and Dad let me do my chores during the week so I could devote my weekends to playing. If I didn't do my chores during the weekdays, I then had to sweep out the garage or clean out my hamster cage during a valuable Saturday when I could have been at the beach with my buddies. In only a couple of weeks I realized the benefits of getting the unpleasant chores out of the way.

The principle has continued in my life. In high school, my friends soon learned that I got my assignments done well before they were due. Why? Because I learned early the value of delayed gratification.

◇ ◇ ◇

Always do right. This will gratify some people, and astonish the rest.
—Mark Twain

◇ ◇ ◇

Of course, this quality can be taken to extremes. We can have too much of this good quality. When I (Les III) was in graduate school, I had a sign over my computer while I was writing my dissertation that said, "Some people spend their entire lives indefinitely preparing to live." This quote by Abraham Maslow referred to the balance we need when trying to delay gratification. The sign hung there for nearly five years and reminded me not to delay too much. There is a time to delay and a time to enjoy. It's all part of teaching the fine art of this important trait.

Why Delayed Gratification Matters

A classic study conducted by Walter Mischel, a psychology professor at Columbia University, offered four-year-old children a choice. The researcher told the children they could have one marshmallow right away. Or if they waited until he returned to the room from a quick errand, they could have two marshmallows instead. He then left the room with a marshmallow left within reach of each four-year-old.

Each of these kids agonized. Some covered their eyes. Some sang. Some gave in. But without knowing it, they had all participated in a test of their willingness to delay gratification.

Researchers kept track of these children during their growing years. The study determined over the years the undisputable power of delayed gratification. Here's the bottom line: children who deferred their gratification for a greater reward in the future emerged later as having far more positive character qualities. They were better adjusted, demonstrated more self-confidence, had wider vocabularies, scored higher on aptitude tests, built better relationships, and eventually secured better jobs than the children who could not put off their desire for an immediate marshmallow to receive two marshmallows a moment later.

This experiment was not designed to say some children are predestined to do better than others. It showed that children who learned to delay their gratification have a greater advantage over children who do not learn to do so.

God's Word seems to agree. Delayed gratification is woven throughout many of the positive personalities we find in scripture. Moses, for example, certainly understood what it meant to replace his self-centered desires with more godly pursuits. "Moses, when he had grown up, refused to be called the son of Pharaoh's daughter; choosing rather to endure ill-treatment with the people of God than to enjoy the passing pleasures of sin" (Heb. 11:24-25, NASB). Noah is another classic example of delayed gratification. "Being warned by God about things not yet seen, . . . prepared an ark for the salvation of his household" (Heb. 11:7, NASB).

Abraham excelled at delayed gratification. Jacob worked seven years for his wife. The teachings of Jesus, especially in the Sermon on the Mount, have multiple references to delayed gratification (see Matt. 5:23-24; 6:33). Almost all of the letters Paul wrote to the young churches were expressions of delayed gratification—until he could visit them in person. And ultimately, the second coming of Christ is an elongated exercise for all believers in delayed gratification.

Does this character trait really matter? More than most people think.

How to Instill This Quality in a Child

You can find dozens of ways to help your child learn to delay gratification. Some involve managing money, some focus on schoolwork, some revolve around doing chores. We'll leave it to you to discover some of the best arenas for this in your home and with your children's personalities. But we're offering some general guiding principles for you to consider as you do so.

◇ ◇ ◇

A healthy self-image is seeing yourself as God sees you—no more and no less.
—Josh McDowell

◇ ◇ ◇

Underscore the value of delay. I (Les III) recently counseled a man in his late 20s whom most would describe as unmotivated and lazy. His parents had given him virtually everything he needed and wanted. He never had to work. On his 16th birthday he received a new sporty car. His parents thought it might help him "fit in" and do better in school. He dropped out before his senior year and, using the trust fund set up by his father, spent most of his time in Colorado on the ski slopes. He had no reason to work and no worries about money.

He visited my office because he felt directionless. He had no idea where he was going with his life. His friends were well into their careers, but he hardly had anything to put on his résumé. Why? Because most of his life, everything had been handed to him. He got what he wanted when he wanted it. He had no comprehension of the word "delay."

Your children may not be at risk of having every financial worry erased from their lives, as my wealthy client did. But if you do not underscore the meaning of delay for your children, they may never learn its value. Show them, through your own actions and examples, how valuable delaying your gratification really is.

Keep your word. In his 1998 book *Lessons from a Father to His Son,* John Ashcroft writes about basketball superstar Michael Jordan. Jordan was never the highest-paid player in the National Basketball Association. When asked why he did not hold out on his contract until he get more money as so many other players do, he replied, "I have always honored my word. I went for security. I had six-year contracts, and I always honored them. People said I was underpaid, but when I signed on the dotted line, I gave my word."

Three years later, after several highly visible players reneged on their contracts, a reporter asked Michael once again about being underpaid. Jordan explained that if his kids saw their dad breaking a promise, he would not be able to continue training them to keep their word. By not asking for a contract renegotiation, Michael Jordan spoke volumes to his children. He told them, "You stand by your word, even when that might go against you." And, as Ashcroft added, his silence became a roar.

Likewise, your children will not be able to ignore the benefits of delayed gratification as they see you keeping your word when you could have taken an easier way out.

◇ ◇ ◇

Seek ye first the kingdom of God . . . and all these things shall be added unto you.
—Matt. 6:33, KJV

◇ ◇ ◇

Model delayed gratification in the little areas. Many years ago, a 10-year-old boy walked to the counter of a soda shop and climbed onto a stool. He caught the eye of the waitress and asked, "How much is an ice-cream sundae?"

"Fifty cents," the waitress replied.

The boy reached into his pockets, pulled out a handful of change, and began counting. Even though the waitress was eager to move on to more prosperous customers who were waiting, he held his ground. "How much is a dish of *plain* ice cream?" he asked.

"Thirty-five cents," she snapped. After counting his money again, the boy ordered the dish of plain ice cream, putting a quarter and two nickels on the counter. The waitress swooped up the coins, brought the ice cream to the boy, and walked away, rolling her eyes.

After the little boy left, the waitress picked up the empty dish and swallowed hard. In a wet spot where the dish had rested sat two nickels and five pennies. The little boy had enough money for a sundae, but chose to forgo that option so he would have enough money left for a tip.

The child probably had seen his mom or dad act in a similar fashion. He had been taught that to leave a tip was the right thing to do. And he put aside his enjoyment to do what was right. A child like this will later be able to apply delayed gratification to the big issues in life as well as the small ones.

Keep your part of the bargain. If, as a parent, you promise your child a bigger reward later for enduring something now, you must deliver the reward. And that prize needs to be worth the wait. Otherwise your child won't be inclined to delay his or her gratification again.

I'll never forget the thud in my stomach when I (Les Sr.) realized I would have to cancel an exciting trip I was going to take with Les III. He was in junior high school, and I had promised to take him with me to Hawaii on a speaking engagement if he could work ahead on his school assignments and get his teachers to approve his weeklong absence.

Les worked furiously to do this. He planned for weeks so he would not be behind in his studies when he returned. He even had arranged a special science project with one teacher that involved collecting lava samples from one of the islands we were to visit. But a day or two before the trip, I became ill. My doctor announced that I needed to stay home.

This was a crushing blow to Les. He had worked so hard. And now he would receive no reward for his hard work. I made up for that the best I could, and we enjoyed another trip together later. But nothing short of illness could have kept me from keeping my part of the bargain. As Dr. Mischel, the researcher with the marshmallows, said, "Unless children learn to believe that it's worth waiting, they won't do it."

So be careful what you promise, and always do your best to keep your word. By the way, the reward should be something your child truly wants, not something you think he or she should want.

DISCUSSION QUESTIONS FOR GROUP STUDY

◆ Did your parents model delayed gratification? How did their practice of this, or lack of practicing this, affect your life?

◆ Think of a time when you practiced delayed gratification. What kind of benefits did this provide in your life?

◆ What qualities does delayed gratification build in our lives? In our spiritual lives?

◆ Brainstorm some ways you can teach your kids at different ages about delayed gratification.

◆ What are some exercises in delayed gratification that you and your kids can experience together?

SEE THE GLASS HALF FULL

◇ ◇ ◇

It is only with the heart that one can see rightly;
what is essential is invisible to the eye.
—Antoine de Saint-Exupèry

ooking across the banquet room, I (Les Sr.) felt a sense of satisfaction as I spotted various people whom I knew had made great effort to attend our fund-raising dinner. All the seats were occupied. Almost everyone seemed animated and happy to be with us. Laughter frequently rose above the table talk.

I was thinking about the pledges we sorely needed when I turned to the chairperson and said, "This is a fine-looking crowd. I believe we'll make our goal."

Without changing his expression, the chairperson responded, "I was just sitting here thinking about all the people who *didn't* come."

Two people visiting Oregon from the East wrote letters on the same March day. One wrote, "It is a beautiful day in Oregon," while the other wrote, "It is the first day we have seen the sun in a month."

Both of them told the truth. But they had different perspectives. One was an optimist, the other a pessimist.

What's the difference between the optimist and the pessimist? It lies in their views of reality. For instance, if you have a glass of water on the shelf and pour out half of it, the optimist will then see the glass as still half full. The pessimist, on the other hand, will see the glass as half empty. They both are correct—they just have differing perspectives.

When the chairman and I were talking about the banquet room crowd, I was seeing the glass as half full, since I noticed all the people who were there. But the chairman was seeing the glass as half empty, thinking of all those who *weren't* there.

Whoever is happy will make others happy too.
—Anne Frank

◇ ◇ ◇

Everything that happens in our private worlds is reviewed by our minds and distilled though our emotions. Only after this automatic two-step process do we decide to focus on the positive prospects or the negative aspects. This makes a world of difference in the kinds of lives we live.

What "Seeing the Glass Half Full" Means

To start a discussion on core values, a youth pastor asked his teenagers, "What would you do if your doctor told you that you had only 24 hours to live?"

The teens mentioned being with friends and family, and the discussion seemed headed in the right direction. But the discussion fell apart when 13-year-old Jason said, "I'd get a second opinion." The kid had optimism.

You might have heard the old story about the shoe salesmen. A shoe factory wanting to expand into a previously undeveloped region sent two marketing scouts to the rough native country to study the prospects for expanding business. One salesmen sent a report back to the home office announcing, "This situation is hopeless. No one wears shoes here."

The other man's report was triumphant: "Glorious business opportunity. Send more representatives and the largest possible shipment as soon as you can. This is a prime territory for customers. No one wears shoes yet!"

Almost everyone looks at life through one of two views: optimism or pessimism. Both are easy to identify. Pessimists usually expect the worst and are prone to depression. Optimists see life in a positive light and view problems as temporary obstacles.

The greatest discovery of my generation is
that a human being can alter his life by
altering his attitudes of mind.
—William James

◇ ◇ ◇

A renowned authority on the subject, Martin Seligman, in his 1998 book *Learned Optimism*, says, "After 25 years of study and research, I am convinced that if we habitually believe, as do the pessimists, that misfortune is our fault, is enduring and will undermine everything we do, more of it will befall us than if we believed otherwise."

In other words, those who see the glass as half empty rather than full will probably lead a life that includes more perceived misfortune.

On the other hand, those who see the glass half full infuse their days with an optimism that engenders positive results from their optimistic thinking. They look for the good in every situation. They find something to be thankful for when others may be wallowing in self-pity. Their outlook is positive, and people around them know it.

I'm glad God has given us the option to choose how we view our world. And I'm glad my parents taught us kids the power of seeing the glass half full.

Why Seeing the Glass Half Full Matters

Optimism matters because without it a person will probably be more likely to suffer significant depression. Mental health professionals note that we are experiencing an epidemic of depression in our country. Depression is 10 times more prevalent today than it was 50 years ago, and it strikes a full 10 years earlier in the life-span than it did in the last generation. This means no age-group is exempt—from children to teenagers to adults to the elderly.

*Attitudes are capable of making the same
experience either pleasant or painful.*
—John Powell

Analysts tell us the problem will also get worse within the next decade or two. Much of it is born of habitual pessimism. For this reason alone, we must teach our children to see the glass half full. But there's more.

Pessimism leads to helplessness. Twenty years ago a University of Pennsylvania experiment involved placing several dogs in a large box with a low wooden divider in the middle. The floor on one side of the divider was electrified with a low voltage device strong enough to activate the dogs, but not strong enough to hurt them. As the shock was administered, most of the dogs jumped over the wooden barrier to the safe floor on the other side. However, a few dogs made no effort to escape but simply lay down on the electrified floor and began to whimper.

At first, the researchers were confounded by the whiners. They were puzzled that these dogs did not jump over the wooden di-vider to avoid the shock. It turned out, however, that the dogs that refused to escape had been used in a former experiment in which the floor on both sides of the divider had been electrified with no escape. Probably feeling helpless, these dogs quit trying. They just dropped to the floor, took the shock, and whimpered. The researchers concluded that they had become victims to learned helplessness. In following years, the researchers found through other experiments that humans who lack optimism are as susceptible to learned helplessness as animals.

◇ ◇ ◇

God . . . gives me the freedom to acknowledge my negative attitudes before him but not the freedom to act them out, because they are as destructive for me as they are for the other person.
—Rebecca Manley Pippert

◇ ◇ ◇

Seeing the glass half full is not important just for what it helps us avoid. It is also important for what it helps us achieve. Consider one example from the business world of sales, described by Martin Seligman in *Learned Optimism.* A large and prestigious insurance company gave a standard test to all prospective salespeople. Those who ranked in the top 50 percent of the test scores were interviewed, and many were hired. However, half of them quit the first year.

The company directors added a standardized test that determined optimism and pessimism. When administrators matched test scores between optimists and pessimists, they found an explanation for this problem. The optimistic salespeople sold 37 percent more than the pessimists, even though they had the same training and sold the same products. Those who scored in the top 10 percent of the optimists sold 88 percent more than the pessimists.

How to Instill This Quality in a Child

"Explanatory style" is how a person views and interprets the world. Experts tell us that this trait develops early in life. As children, we learn to explain incidents on the playground, for example, or circumstances in the home to ourselves. These views become entrenched early in life as we develop habits for explaining why certain things happen. And those explanations tend to be mostly optimistic or mostly pessimistic. Here are some strategies you can use to help if your child falls into the more pessimistic camp.

Don't let the little things get big. According to the United States Bureau of Standards, a dense fog covering seven city blocks to a depth of a hundred feet contains less liquid than one glass of water.

At times we let a small amount of worry fog up our entire "visual" field. One little incident, such as a negative remark by a stranger, can ruin an entire day for some people. A poor grade on a quiz at school may cause a child to doubt his or her intellectual ability. Like fog, our worries can thoroughly block our vision of the light of God's promises. But also like fog, our worries often have very little real substance to them.

Think of it as being easy, and it shall be easy. Think of it as being difficult, and it shall be difficult.
—Arabian proverb

Help kids look at things realistically and determine situations rather than just panicking.

Look for what others don't readily see. Inspirational speaker and writer Barbara Johnson tells of a woman whose day was not going well. She had overslept and was late for work. Her deadlines at the office contributed to her harried condition. By the time she reached the bus stop for her trip home, her stomach was tied in a knot. The bus was late and packed, so she had to stand for the whole trip home. As Barbara puts it, "The day wasn't improving even as it came to an end."

Then the woman heard a man's voice rise from the front of the bus. "Beautiful day, isn't it?" he asked. Because of the crowd, she couldn't see the man, but she continued to hear his voice commenting on everything the bus passed that added to his joy: a church here, an ice-cream store there, a baseball diamond here, a library there. The bus passengers began to loosen up and enjoy the ride, including this woman. The man's enthusiasm was so winsome that the woman began to smile. When the bus reached the woman's stop, she worked her way through the crowd to the door and, near the front of the bus, discovered the "tour guide"—a man wearing dark glasses and carrying a white cane. He was blind.

As the woman stepped off of the bus, she realized that God had used a blind man to help her see the glass half full. You can do the same thing for your child by pointing out good things on even the most disappointing days.

◇ ◇ ◇

Your living is determined not so much by what life brings to you as by the attitude you bring to life; not so much by what happens to you as by the way your mind looks at what happens.

—John Homer Miller

◇ ◇ ◇

Give thanks in all things. In *The Hiding Place*, Corrie ten Boom tells about an incident that taught her the principle of giving thanks in all things. During World War II, the ten Boom family harbored Jewish people in their home. Eventually they were discovered and arrested. Corrie and her sister, Betsie, were sent to the Ravensbruck concentration camp.

The barracks building they lived in was overcrowded and infested with fleas. Corrie hated the crowding. Most of all, she hated the fleas. One morning Corrie and Betsie read in their tattered

Bible the I Thess. 5:18 reminder to rejoice in all things: "Give thanks in all circumstances, for this is God's will for you in Christ Jesus."

Betsie said, "Corrie, we've got to give thanks for this barracks and even for these fleas."

Corrie replied, "I cannot thank God for fleas." But Betsie was persuasive, and reluctantly, Corrie did thank God even for the fleas.

During the following months, Corrie and Betsie found that the guards tended to avoid their barracks. This was odd, because the guards were constantly breathing down the necks of the women in the other buildings. Because the women in Corrie and Betsie's barracks were left relatively free, Corrie and Betsie could lead a Bible study, talk openly about Christianity, and even pray in the barracks. It became their place of refuge. Several months later they learned that the reason the guards never entered their barracks was because of those irritating fleas. And because the barracks was overcrowded, Betsie and Corrie were able to share the message of God's love with more women.

I am an old man and have known a great many troubles, but most of them never happened.
—Mark Twain

Corrie's story is a powerful reminder of how the attitude of gratitude can lift us out of a miserable experience. And while most of us will never have to endure such inhuman conditions, we will encounter times when we have every right to be discouraged and downhearted. But in those times we can model the ability to adjust to things beyond our control. And when children see Mom or Dad do this, they remember it for a long time. So don't discount the lessons you teach your children about this quality when you give thanks in all things.

Discussion Questions for Group Study

◆ Is it always good to be an optimist?

◆ Do you tend to see the glass as half full or half empty?

◆ How can we teach kids to be realistic about their fears without being insensitive to their fears and feelings?

◆ Can you recall a time when you gave thanks even though the circumstances looked bad? How did it turn out? What did you learn through the situation?

◆ When your child has a negative outlook, what can you do to help his or her attitude?

5

BITE YOUR TONGUE WHEN NECESSARY

◇ ◇ ◇

Rest satisfied with doing well,
and leave others to talk of you as they please.
—Pythagoras

When I (Les III) was in the third grade, Dad and I read together about the myths attached to Paul Bunyan's life. He was a legendary woodsman from the headwaters of the Mississippi River in Minnesota. According to the stories, he was larger and more powerful than any other man in the woods. His voice made the birds stop singing and the leaves tremble. Everyone did what he commanded—except one man.

One woodsman constantly spouted critical attitudes and streams of profanity that grated on the nerves of even rough-hewn lumbermen who usually didn't notice expletives.

Paul Bunyan commanded this woodsman to stop his critical ways, but it did no good. Bunyan then turned to physical persuasion. Although he pummeled the offender mercilessly, the man's language did not change. Paul Bunyan begged, cajoled, threatened, bribed, and called on every means he knew to stop the terrible bursts of offensive language, but to no avail. Then something happened that changed everything.

One winter it got cold enough in Minnesota to send the thermometer mercury through the bottom of the ball to immeasurable degrees of cold—far below zero on the Fahrenheit scale. The extreme cold froze each word in the air as it was spoken. Watching these frozen words drop to the ground gave Paul Bunyan an idea. He directed his helpers to gather and stack all of the frozen words of the offensive lumberman until spring arrived. When the bitter cold of winter moved into the warming rays of the sun and the temperatures began to rise above zero toward the melting zone, Paul Bunyan made the lumberman sit down and listen to every expletive he had uttered all winter. According to the story, the man never said a critical word again.

The Paul Bunyan story is myth. But one report I read discussed the potential to retrieve words that are still floating around in the universe. Some scientists say technological breakthroughs may give us the ability to reach into the air and pull in speeches and conversations that set airwaves in motion hundreds or even thousands of years ago. Theoretically, the words of Lincoln at Gettysburg, or those of our Lord in the Sermon on the Mount, are still floating around in the cosmos.

Impossible as this idea sounds, it is both magnificent and frightening. Many things are said that are better forgotten, but words have a life of their own. Once spoken, they can never be unspoken. And when we listen to ourselves, we sometimes hear what we do not like. Too often our conversations are weighed with quick-frozen criticisms, and only lightly sprinkled with compliments.

What "Biting Your Tongue" Means

On a hot August day in the 1970s, Alexander Butterfield dropped a bomb in the Watergate hearings by reporting that the Oval Office of the White House in Washington, D.C., was bugged with sophisticated sound recording equipment. An emotional tidal wave swept over the entire country. The lead story on the television news that night was this terrible thing the United States president had done by bugging the Oval Office. The next editions of the *Washington Post, New York Times, Chicago Tribune, Boston Globe,* and all other daily newspapers, great and small, featured bold black banners about the president's office being bugged. Bugging became a national obsession. Most of the time when two people met on national talk shows or at the counters of coffeehouses, they discussed the tapes. All public and private conversations led to the West Wing of the White House. Were the tapes his or someone else's? If they were his, why did he not destroy them? If they were ours, why couldn't we hear them? What happened to the crucial 18 minutes of tape that mysteriously disappeared from its reel? Bugging talk even entered the routine of the television comedians. I (Les Sr.) remember hearing one comedian say the president had celebrated the vice president's birthday by sending him 12 long-stemmed microphones.

Wise men talk because they have something to say; fools, because they have to say something.
—Plato

The appropriateness of bugging became an issue at our house. Halfway through a formal meal at the dining room table, I heard a strange clicking coming from the centerpiece. Then Les III pulled a microphone from the floral arrangement and triumphantly reported that he had bugged the table conversation. Then he insisted that we all sit there and listen to what we had said, especially about him.

That experience made our family think. What would it be like if each of us bugged ourselves and then listened to our own conversations? What would it be like to hear again all the things we have said in the past 24 hours? In short, we began to ask, "If you bugged yourself, what would you hear?" And that question gets to the heart of this chapter. When we talk about biting your tongue as a character quality, we're talking about becoming aware of our own words and editing out unhelpful comments.

That's not easy to do. As James 3:2 says, "We all stumble in many ways. If anyone is never at fault in what he says, he is a perfect man, able to keep his whole body in check." But learning to discipline our speech is necessary if we're to pass a legacy of love to our children.

Why "Biting Your Tongue" Matters

Shortly after midnight on Saturday, April 26, 1986, workers were performing routine maintenance at the Chernobyl nuclear power plant in the northeast corner of the Ukraine. Suddenly an uncontrolled power surge raced through reactor No. 4, producing steam and hydrogen, which culminated in a massive explosion. A mile-high nuclear cloud hovered for 10 days over much of the Soviet Union and Europe, releasing its nuclear rain.

Live with men as if God saw you,
and talk to God as if men were listening.
—Athenodorus

In the summer of 1993 I (Les III) witnessed the devastation this accident brought to this region and its people. On a humanitarian assignment for World Vision International, I was sent to Chernobyl to help those who had not been amenable to physical healing. I walked around an abused landscape that will require many thousands of years to heal. I talked with the suffering children. The children were affected most because most had been outside in the acid rain; and because their bodies are smaller, they ingested a larger percentage of the poison. As a result, a high percentage of them ended up with forms of cancer from these hazardous chemicals.

Besides talking with these hurting children, I listened to their desperate parents. I met with courageous doctors, and I saw what life was like in Chernobyl's "dead zone." Life will never again be simple and uncomplicated for 2 million residents of Belarus. Because the chemical rain soaked into their earth, their food supply is even still affected. These people are still exposed daily to off-the-chart levels of radiation.

Reflecting upon my heartrending experience in Chernobyl's contaminated region and continuing my work as a psychotherapist with troubled families in the United States, I have come to a fresh realization: as soil and air are poisoned by radiation, so the human heart and mind are poisoned by critical attitudes.

Honest criticism is hard to take, particularly from a relative, a friend, an acquaintance, or a stranger.
—Franklin P. Jones

In some homes words are used as weapons to crush the human spirit. These verbal missiles attack almost anything attached to a person—possessions, behavior, appearance, intelligence, or even the total value of their personhood. James wrote that "[the human tongue is] full of deadly poison" (James 3:8, NASB).

As radiation sickness destroys the immune system, toxic words destroy the spirit. In extreme form, this use of toxic words is called verbal abuse. It rains through such statements as "You'll never amount to anything," "Can't you do anything right?" and "You're the most disgusting little creep who ever walked the face of the earth."

Verbal abuse, many experts claim, is just as destructive as physical abuse. Both bring emotional devastation.

Verbal toxicity, however, is often dispensed in subtle forms. We sometimes camouflage our criticism in what we claim is humor. People wiggle out of being held accountable for cruel statements by saying, "I was only joking." Or we shoot a poisonous dart with "helpful" advice that's actually an artful put-down. Sometimes we withhold our attention to express our disapproval. Regardless of its form, criticism poisons the human spirit much like a nuclear disaster poisons a landscape.

How to Instill This Quality in a Child

Since the pain of being criticized is universal, I'm endlessly surprised that most of us are so quick to criticize others—even the people who are closest to us. We seem to have an irresistible urge to find fault. Pascal said, "We find fault with perfection itself." That's the reason our suggestions for instilling this quality in a child are focused so heavily on how you can model nontoxic talk.

Separate the person from the behavior. Your child must see you recognize that what people *do* does not equal who they *are.* This requires a great deal of diligence on your part. If you aren't doing this already, begin by placing your focus on what other people do rather than who you see them to be. In other words, describe their actions, not their character. A good technique for doing this can be to talk with adverbs (which describe a person's actions) rather than adjectives (which describe a person's qualities). Thus, when talking to your child about someone at work (or, even more importantly, when you know your child is eavesdropping on a conversation you are having with another adult) you might say a person "talked a great deal in the meeting," rather than that this person "is a loudmouth."

Make critiques helpful, not hurtful. At times we need to give constructive guidance. You will certainly find it necessary to confront your child about irresponsible behavior. But how you express corrective guidance makes all the difference in whether your child listens and acts on it. Henry Ward Beecher said, "No man can tell another his faults so as to benefit him, unless he loves him."

The point is not to avoid critical thinking and simply accept everything without value judgments. The point is to make our critiques helpful—and not damage a person's self-image in the process. The apostle Paul understood this when he wrote: "Therefore let us stop passing judgment on one another. Instead, *make up your mind* not to put any stumbling block or obstacle in your brother's way" (Rom. 14:13, italics mine). Practice sharing your feelings without putting a stumbling block in your child's way.

If you can't say anything nice . . . Perhaps your mother drilled the saying into your brain too: "If you can't say anything nice, don't say anything at all." That quip is good for us to put into practice when we're dealing with our own kids.

When we advance a little in life, we find that the tongue of man creates nearly all the mischief of the world.
—Paxton Hood

Heaven knows that children can be frustrating to deal with at any age. Sometimes as we get caught up in those maddening moments, we can be tempted to let loose and say exactly what we're thinking. At times like that, when we can't control our tongues, it's best to say nothing at all. That may seem impossible to do—especially when our words would be true, or when our children have definitely provoked us. Remember: Nothing is wrong with getting distance between you and your child until you regain control of your mouth. It's always valid to say, "You know, I can't talk to you about this right now. We're going to have to discuss it later."

Love means sometimes having to say you're sorry. The perfect person is able to hold his or her tongue at all times. What happens if we're not perfect? Let your children see that you know you're not perfect—apologize for speaking wrongly, for losing your temper, for saying unkind words.

Our children understand the problem of being tempted to say hurtful things, and the temptation of speaking in anger. When we admit we were wrong, that we sinned, we don't erase the wrong words we've spoken—they'll still have consequences and aren't to be taken lightly. But we show our children the right example by asking for their forgiveness when we've hurt them or wronged them with our words.

Likewise, we can help our children learn to be kind by teaching them to apologize when their tongues are undisciplined. Even when they speak wrongly to us, it's still appropriate to ask for their apology.

To speak kindly does not hurt the tongue.
—French proverb

◇ ◇ ◇

Another thing we can do as parents is to point out when people are speaking inappropriately. If a character on a television show you're watching with your child is rude, don't just shrug off the incident—talk to your kids about it. Too many statistics show the influence that music, movies, and TV can have on children when their parents don't counter the wrong attitudes and words of the media.

Help your kids see the good in others. Most parents of public school kids have felt the very hairs rise on the back of their necks as they hear their children relate the things that are spoken in the halls of learning. Kindness and controlled speech are not taught by many parents these days. So how can we help our children keep from saying ugly things about others?

Start a discussion with your kids about some of the things their friends say to others. Ask them how the person who was being verbally abused felt. Ask them how they would feel if someone else said that to them.

We can also help our children by teaching them how much

God values each of us. I John 4:21 tells us that "whoever loves God must also love his brother." Talk to your children about how we treat the people we love—and how we're to treat everyone in that same way.

You can also remind your kids to look for the good in others. When we find admirable traits, even in unlovely people, we are taking the first step in learning to care for them.

DISCUSSION QUESTIONS FOR GROUP STUDY

◆ What are some biblical examples of people whose tongues ran away with them?

◆ Can you talk about a time someone's words hurt you?

◆ Can you think of a time you were convicted for speaking wrongly? What did you do about it?

◆ When are you most tempted to use words with your kids that aren't Christlike?

◆ Make a list of kind, affirming things you can say to your children.

PRACTICE TOTAL COMMITMENT

Do every act of your life as if it were your last.
—Marcus Aurelius

Some years ago, while Les III was still in high school, I flew from Chicago to Phoenix for a weekend seminar. During the Saturday lunch break, a businessman handed me a book and said, "I think you'll find this interesting." He suggested I return the book to him on Sunday morning at church.

I didn't get around to looking at the book until bedtime.

Ordinarily, I would have read a few minutes and dropped off to sleep. But the book was so captivating, I read into the night, long after my lights should have been out. The next morning, when I saw the book's owner in the church foyer, I told him I was not ready to give up the book. I saw the price of the book on the jacket. And I had the money out of my pocket, ready to give him. He refused the money and told me to keep the book. I finished the book on the plane that afternoon between Phoenix and Chicago.

Around bedtime, when I arrived at our home in Illinois, I walked directly to the room where Les III was working on his studies. I put the book on his desk and proposed, "If you'll read this book and write me a report so I know you understand it, I'll give you $10." Since Les was at the age where he would do anything for $10, he agreed without any questions or qualifications.

That book episode happened years ago. Les never wrote the report, and I never gave him the $10. But we've talked about Robert Shook's premise in *Total Commitment* scores of times. And that is no exaggeration.

The premise of the book is disarmingly simple: Any one of us can achieve almost any goal we set for ourselves if only we have total and absolute commitment. High achievements are not most generated by a high IQ, impressive technical skills, or conceptual thinking, but by total and absolute commitment. That premise is so basic, so fundamental, it has long since been absorbed as a trait in our family. And this is a trait we believe is critical to helping our children live fulfilling lives of purpose.

What "Practicing Total Commitment" Means

A Haitian parable illustrates total commitment to Christ this way: A man wanted to sell his house for $2,000. Another man badly wanted to buy it but couldn't afford the full price. After much bargaining, the owner agreed to sell the house for half the original price with one stipulation: he would retain ownership of one small nail protruding from just over the door. After several years the original owner wanted the house back, but the new owner was unwilling to sell. So the first owner hung the carcass of a dead dog from the nail he still owned. Soon the house became unlivable, and the family was forced to sell the house to the owner of the nail.

What does this have to do with total commitment? The point of the parable is simple. If we leave the devil one small area in our life, he will return to hang his rotting garbage on it, making it unfit for Christ's indwelling. Total commitment, whether in our relationship to Christ, to our work, to our family, or to anything else, means dedicating every aspect of our beings to the goals we have set.

Consider another aspect that helps explain this quality. It has to do with knowing where you're headed even when your eventual goal seems far away. In a very real sense, total commitment means pressing on even when you can't see the finish line.

United States runner Marla Runyon is a good example. She has been legally blind for 22 years. Even so, she competed in the 2000 Summer Olympic Games in Sydney, Australia. In fact, she qualified for the finals in the 1500-meter race. Not only that, Marla finished eighth, three seconds behind the medal winners. How does she do it? Marla can't see in color, and what she does see is just a fuzzy blob. In a race she just follows the blob of figures in front of her. She told television commentator Tom Hammonds that her real difficulty was in rounding the final turn and "racing toward a finish line that I can't see. I just know where it is." That's total commitment!

◇ ◇ ◇

Behold the turtle. He makes progress only
when he sticks his neck out.
—James B. Conant

◇ ◇ ◇

The apostle Paul wrote to the Philippians, "But one thing I do: Forgetting what is behind and straining toward what is ahead, I press on toward the goal to win the prize for which God has called me heavenward in Christ Jesus" (Phil. 3:13-14).

Paul was talking about total commitment. Total commitment requires that we forget the past and move ahead toward the prize of the future.

Why This Quality Matters

Can you imagine what would happen if all of the married couples in America suddenly were totally committed to their marriages? The future of divorce courts and the careers of divorce lawyers would be threatened, to say the least.

Can you imagine what would happen to North American culture if each citizen suddenly was absolutely committed to honesty? Instead of needing to hire 100,000 new police officers, our police forces would need to furlough a large portion of officers.

Can you imagine what would happen if every student, at any

level, in our school systems—from first grade through graduate school—was absolutely committed to his or her studies? We would be closer to having a generation of near geniuses. And we would certainly have a generation of more self-confident, capable people.

Total commitment raises the level of life. It is the fuel in the tank of every human who has ever achieved anything worthwhile. Consider all that we would have missed if people listened to critics and did not cultivate total commitment on the way to achieving their goals:

- The director of the United States Patent Office said, "Everything that can be invented has been invented"—in 1899.
- The president of England's Royal Society said in 1885, "Heavier-than-air flying machines are impossible." Guess the Wright brothers weren't listening.
- Tris Spaeker told Babe Ruth that he had made a big mistake when he gave up pitching to focus on batting.
- 402 banks turned down Walt Disney before he got a loan to build his amusement park in California.

That last fact is mind-blowing. Can you imagine the total commitment that Walt Disney had to his vision for a theme park to keep trying after so many financial rejections? As we said, this quality is the fuel in the tank of every human being who has ever achieved anything worthwhile.

How to Instill This Quality in a Child

The great saboteur of instilling total commitment in a child centers around the phrase "Someday I'll . . ."

This phrase denotes idle thinking that is rarely backed by action. And most well-intentioned people regularly utter it. But to teach a child the fine art of total commitment, we need to move beyond the daydreams of "Someday I'll . . ." Instead, we need to start living our dreams in the present. Here are a few pointers for doing that.

Avoid excuses. Motivational speaker and writer Zig Ziglar tells of a man who went next door to borrow his neighbor's lawnmower.

The neighbor explained that the man could not use the mower because all the flights had been canceled from New York to Los Angeles. The would-be borrower asked him what canceled flights from New York to Los Angeles had to do with borrowing the lawnmower.

"It doesn't have anything to do with it," the neighbor replied. "But if I don't want to let you use my lawnmower, one excuse is as good as another."

◇ ◇ ◇

Hell is to drift, heaven is to steer.
—George Bernard Shaw

◇ ◇ ◇

Some people go through life day after day, piling one excuse on top of another. They look for any reason to avoid working at their goals. If you want your child to avoid the trap of making excuses, begin by paying attention to the excuses you make and how your child might be following in your footsteps. This is a quality that is caught as much as it is taught.

Then help your child to have the courage to move beyond excuses.

Set goals. If you seriously want to help your child cultivate total commitment, help him or her set goals. Of course, these goals need to be reachable and appropriate for the child's age. But don't be afraid to start young. Even a three-year-old can benefit from a simple short-term goal such as putting up toys before being allowed to watch a Barney video.

But as a child matures, the goals can become more long-term and require more work. Remember that as your child reaches a goal, he or she must receive a reward for all of his or her effort. That reward is usually best chosen by the child. Saving money for a bike the child wants is an example. With this goal of a new bike in mind, the child will have to weigh each financial decision. Does he or she really want to buy that candy bar that looks so good, or does the child want to put that money toward the bike? When your children set goals, they face decisions like these and they learn to be committed to their goals.

Man who says "it cannot be done" should not interrupt man who is doing it.
—Chinese proverb

◇ ◇ ◇

Practice perseverance. All the goals in the world mean nothing if a person does not have the stick-to-it attitude to make them materialize. In his compelling book *Me: The Narcissistic American,* psychoanalyst Aaron Stern gets right to the point: "To attain emotional maturity, each of us must learn to develop . . . the ability to delay immediate gratification in favor of long-range goals." With this in mind, you may want to review the earlier chapter in this book on delaying gratification—it has a lot to do with practicing total commitment.

We can help our children develop perseverance by having them stick to tasks. For instance, 17-year-old Nicole has a tough time sticking to tasks. When the going gets tough, she tends to quit. As you might guess, this has resulted in bad grades, incomplete goals, and unrealized dreams when Nicole is not willing to do the work involved to make her dreams come true. She hasn't yet learned that gain often means pain.

Nicole's parents are working with her to help her achieve little goals—such as in reading. Nicole does poorly in her American literature class because any time she gets bored with the subject or the text becomes a bit laborious to read, she zones out and stops trying. Her parents are helping her learn concentration in reading by teaching her to set goals—like reading a simple book all the way through and offering a reward when she completes the book.

Sometimes Nicole decides the reward isn't worth the work and stops trying. At such times, her mom and dad have to step in with their good old parental authority and make rules, withholding privileges (like talking on the phone to her boyfriend) until she finishes the task at hand. As she practices perseverance to complete simple tasks and gets used to finishing jobs, she builds her "perseverance strength" much as an athlete in training builds his or her strength by repeated exercise. This perseverance will help her build commitment.

Be proactive. It's so easy to be passive—to move through life simply reacting to outside forces. Like passengers on a bumpy bus ride, we watch the scenery flash by our window as life happens around us. We show up, sit back, and let outer circumstances determine our destination. Most of us plan more for a Christmas party than we do for our lives!

But when it comes to cultivating total commitment, we need to get active. John Hancock said, "All worthwhile people have good thoughts, good ideas, and good intentions, but precious few of them ever translate those into action." It's impossible to have commitment and not be doing something about it.

After we set goals, we must put the wheels into motion by planning how to achieve those goals. We need to make sure our plans for reaching these goals are attainable and realistic.

Make sacrifices. One of the most effective ways to teach total commitment to a child is to let him or her see the sacrifices you make in order to achieve your goals. For example, if your church is holding a special campaign to build a new sanctuary, let your child see the sacrifices you make financially to help with the building program. Let the child see you skip a meal at a restaurant in order to save the money for the building fund. And let your child participate in the process. Let him or her find ways to be a part—like pledging part of his or her allowance for several months or doing without treats to put the money toward the new building.

Be careful, however, to avoid motivating your kids through guilt. Make sure they see that a good sacrifice is done for good reasons, not simply to alleviate guilt. Teach them to see the positive trade-off for the sacrifice. In the instance of the church, lead your kids in a discussion on how the congregation will benefit from the new facility. Then bring it to a personal level, and let your kids note how they personally will benefit—maybe the new church will have better Sunday School rooms or a gym. Maybe the sanctuary will be more comfortable. Maybe they'll enjoy services enhanced by new sound or lighting equipment.

DISCUSSION QUESTIONS FOR GROUP STUDY

◆ Give an example of someone you know who displays total commitment in an area of his or her life. What marks that commitment?

◆ What kind of sacrifices does commitment to parenting involve?

◆ What kinds of things would you like your children to be totally committed to? How can you help them realize your dreams for them?

◆ Can you think of a time when you used excuses and ended up not achieving your goals?

◆ Remember a time when you've been totally committed to something (perhaps it was a total commitment to win your spouse's heart before you were married)—how did that commitment affect your actions?

BUILD
RELATIONSHIPS
THAT ENDURE

We cannot live only for ourselves.
A thousand fibers connect us with our fellow men;
and among those fibers, as sympathetic threads,
our actions run as causes, and they come back to us as effects.
—Herman Melville

or five months Navy Admiral Richard Byrd survived "one layer of darkness piled on top of the other." He lived in a feeble shelter on the Ross Ice Barrier near the south pole, enduring the "coldest cold on the face of the earth." The terrain was a sheet of ice thousands of feet thick with mounds of powdery snow shifting across its threatening surface. The temperature often dropped to 80 degrees below zero. In mid-April the sun dipped below the horizon and didn't return for weeks. The explorer suffered frostbite, monoxide poisoning, disturbed sleep, and malnutrition.

When Admiral Byrd returned to civilization and wrote an account of his exploration, the title of his book did not emphasize the terrain, the weather, the danger, the darkness, or the sickness.

A single word underscored the horror of being isolated from other people—*alone.*

But you don't have to suffer arctic cold to feel alone and neglected. Loneliness is common in populous and bustling communities. It is one of the heaviest weights the human heart can endure. That's why building relationships that endure is so critical to helping our children live fulfilled lives.

What "Building Relationships That Endure" Means

The anguish of loneliness is better defined by experience than a dictionary. It is being the last fifth grader chosen in a game of pickup baseball. It is living in a hectic home and never hearing a kind word of affirmation. It is visiting a crowded shopping center and longing to share the experience with *anybody.*

To underscore this important quality, consider a recent survey of more than 40,000 people of all ages. The survey found that 67 percent of people feel lonely some of the time. Another study showed that loneliness is a serious personal problem for as many as 25 percent of the population. Feeling alone and neglected is an emotional epidemic flooding the lives of millions of Americans. In one year the average American today probably meets as many people as the average person met in a whole lifetime 100 years ago. And yet we are far lonelier. The feeling of being alone, however, does not necessarily need to result in our or our children's feeling isolated—once we learn the lessons of building enduring relationships.

And what are these enduring relationships? They are connections with people who speak our language, who understand our hearts, and who share our passions. These are relationships with people who not only help us escape the bitter cold of loneliness but also help us become better people just by our being around them.

Why Building Relationships That Endure Matters

A pioneering band of researchers recently studied the age-old mystery of what makes people happy. Their answer is not what you might expect. What consistently rises to the top of the charts is not success, good looks, or any similar enviable assets. The clear winner is relationships. Close ones. People are happiest when they have good relationships.

◇ ◇ ◇

It is one of the most beautiful compensations of life that no one can sincerely try to help another without helping himself.
—Ralph Waldo Emerson

◇ ◇ ◇

Rick, a sophomore in high school, didn't make the football team. His parents had no plans to buy him a car. He wasn't the best-looking kid in his class or the smartest. But Rick was happy. What was Rick's secret? He had discovered a truth that many unhappy adults never learn: Few things can make a person feel better in life than building a good relationship.

Or consider another example. In Brooklyn, Chush is a school that caters to learning-disabled children. Some children remain in Chush for their entire school career, while others can be mainstreamed into conventional schools. At a fund-raising dinner, the father of a Chush child delivered an unforgettable speech.

After extolling the school and its dedicated staff, he cried out, "Where is the perfection in my son Shaya? Everything God does is done with perfection. But my child cannot understand things as other children do. My child cannot remember facts and figures as other children do. Where is God's perfection?"

The audience was shocked by the question, pained by the father's anguish over his learning-disabled son, and stilled by the piercing query.

"I believe," the father answered, "that when God brings a child like this into the world, the perfection He seeks is in the way people react to this child."

He then told an astounding story about his son Shaya: One afternoon Shaya and his father walked past a park where some boys Shaya knew were playing baseball. Shaya asked, "Do you think they'll let me play?"

Shaya's father knew that his son was not at all athletic and that most boys would not want him on their team. But Shaya's father understood that if his son were chosen to play, it would give him a comfortable sense of belonging; so he approached a boy in the field and asked if Shaya could play. The boy looked around for guidance from his teammates. Getting none, he took matters into his own hands and said, "We're losing by six runs, and the game's in the eighth inning. I guess he can be on our team, and we'll try to put him up to bat in the ninth inning."

Shaya's father was ecstatic as Shaya smiled broadly. Shaya was told to put on a glove and to go out to play short center field. In the bottom of the eighth inning, Shaya's team scored a few runs but was still behind by three. In the bottom of the ninth inning, Shaya's team scored again. Now, with two outs and the bases loaded with the potential winning run on base, Shaya was scheduled to be up. Would the team actually let him bat and potentially give away their chance to win the game?

Surprisingly, Shaya was given the bat. Everyone knew that it was nearly impossible for Shaya's team to win the game at this point because he didn't even know how to hold the bat properly, let alone hit with it. However, as he stepped to the plate, the pitcher moved a few steps forward. He lobbed the ball in softly so Shaya should at least be able to make contact. The first pitch came, and Shaya swung clumsily and missed.

One of Shaya's teammates came up to him, and together they held the bat and faced the pitcher waiting for the next pitch. The pitcher again took a few steps forward to toss the ball softly toward him. As the pitch came in, Shaya and his teammate swung at the ball, and together they hit a slow ground ball to the pitcher.

The pitcher picked up the soft grounder and could easily have thrown the ball to the first baseman. Shaya would have been out, and that would have ended the game. Instead, the pitcher took the ball and threw it in a high arc to right field, far beyond the reach of the first baseman. Everyone started yelling, "Shaya, run to first! Run to first!"

Never in his life had Shaya run to first. He scampered down the baseline wide-eyed and startled. By the time he reached first base, the right fielder had the ball. He could have thrown the ball to the second-base guy, who would tag out Shaya, who was still running. But the right fielder understood the pitcher's intentions, so he threw the ball high and far over the third baseman's head. Everyone yelled, "Run to second! Run to second!"

Shaya ran toward second base as the runners ahead of him circled the bases toward home. As he reached second base, the opposing shortstop ran to him, turned him in the direction of third base, and shouted, "Run to third!"

As Shaya rounded third, the boys from both teams ran behind him, screaming, "Shaya, run home!" Shaya ran home, stepped on home plate, and all 18 boys lifted him onto their shoulders and pronounced him the hero—he had just hit a "grand slam" and won the game for his team.

"That day," said the father softly with tears now rolling down his face, "those 18 boys reached their level of God's perfection."

I love this story, because it illustrates boys putting a person ahead of winning a game. And that's what we have to do if we want to build enduring relationships. We have to be willing to put others ahead of our programs, ahead of our plans. As we value them and let them see us value them, we find a priceless treasure of love.

How to Instill This Quality in a Child

What can you do to build good relationships? To be honest, the answer is "not much." You can't *do* a whole lot to cultivate healthy relationships. Techniques don't work. Real relationships evolve out of *being* a certain kind of person. So our pointers in this chapter focus on cultivating traits rather than techniques. The goal is to help your children spotlight *who* they are in relationships rather than what they *do*.

*Life's most persistent and urgent question
is: What are you doing for others?*
—Martin Luther King Jr.

◇ ◇ ◇

Be someone who listens. Good relationships develop when a person is able to listen and understand what another person is saying. If we don't accurately listen to another person, we can't build a good relationship with him or her. Help your children be the kind of people who take the time to hear what others are saying. Teach your kids not to interrupt or jump to conclusions in their communication. Show them how to patiently let the other person say what is on his or her mind. As your children mature, teach them to become like a mirror reflecting an image—they can reflect the person's message by saying something like, "What I hear you saying is . . ." This kind of a reflection lets the person know your kids are really interested in accurately understanding him or her, and it does wonders to build enduring relationships.

Be someone who is safe. A close relationship is built on feelings of security. If a person doesn't feel safe with you, there's no hope of him or her ever opening up and being authentic. Creating a sense of security for people in relationship includes a couple of elements. One way of offering "safety" is to offer acceptance. Our friends need to feel we will always accept them. Even when they say or do something that's wrong, we must clearly let them know we love them and accept them. Our kids see us display this quality as we love them for who they are, regardless of what they *do.*

To create a sense of security for people in relationship, we must also keep our word. Of course, this is something that is better "caught" than taught. Your child needs to see you live this trait in your life. If you promise to do a favor for your kids, do it. If you promise to keep a secret, keep it. Be a person of your word. When you have earned your children's trust, they are more likely to become trustworthy, and their relationships will flourish for decades.

Be someone who lends a hand. In rewarding relationships, people not only enjoy feelings of security but also help each other out. Sometimes that help is tangible, like helping your child with homework. And sometimes this help may come in the form of giving your kids reassurance before they take a test they've studied hard for. The point is that your child needs to learn to help others because he or she wants to, not out of being forced. And this lesson can be learned earlier than you think.

Intimate relationships cannot substitute for a life plan. But to have any meaning or viability at all, a life plan must include intimate relationships.
—Harriet Lerner

Consider the story Jack Kelley, foreign affairs editor for *USA Today,* told a crowd of Christian magazine editors at the Evangelical Press Association convention:

We were in Mogadishu, the capital of Somalia, in East Africa, during a famine. It was so bad we walked into one village and everybody was dead. We saw this little boy. You could tell he had worms and was malnourished. Our photographer had a grapefruit, which he gave to the boy. The boy was so weak he didn't have the strength to hold the grapefruit, so we cut it in half and gave it to him. He picked it up, looked at us as if to say thanks, and walked back toward his village. We walked behind him where he couldn't see us. When he entered the village, on the ground was a little boy whom I thought was dead. His eyes were completely glazed over. It turned out that this was the boy's younger brother. The older brother knelt next to his younger brother, bit off a piece of the grapefruit, and chewed it. Then he opened his younger brother's mouth, put the grapefruit in, and worked his brother's jaw up and down. We learned that the older brother had been doing that for the younger brother for two weeks. A couple days later the older brother died of malnutrition, and the younger brother lived. I remember driving home that night thinking, *I wonder if this is what Jesus meant when He said, "There is no greater love than to lay down our life for somebody else."*

◇ ◇ ◇

Love consists in this, that two solitudes protect and touch and greet each other.
—Rainer Maria Rilke

◇ ◇ ◇

Whether our acts of service and help are lifesaving or just helping someone save time or frustration, assisting others with their needs brings joy to life. We can teach our kids not only to be people who pitch in and help when something needs to be done but also to be people who look for ways to help others.

Be someone who walks in another's shoes. To build good relationships, you must learn to see the world from another person's perspective. The technical word for this is "empathy." And when we feel empathy, we can unlock a million mysteries. When we put ourselves in another person's shoes, we begin to understand why he or she might react, feel, and think as he or she does. Of course, empathizing with others does not come naturally. Help your child put this quality into practice by suggesting that he or she consider what somebody else might be thinking or feeling in various circumstances. For instance, when your child complains about the way another kid has acted at school, you can ask, "Do you have any idea why he [she] might have done that?" Your child might respond, "I think he [she] might have been mad because I was talking to his girlfriend [her boyfriend]."

"Hmm—how do you think you'd feel if he [she] had been talking with your girlfriend [boyfriend]?" you might reply. "Would you have been jealous?"

"No, if I were him [her], I'd know I wasn't about to try to steal his girlfriend [her boyfriend]," your child would probably say.

"Must be tough to be so afraid you're going to lose your girlfriend [boyfriend]," you could say. That would help your child start thinking about why people act the way they do. Or if a child complains, you could say, "Does this person normally act like this, or do you think something's wrong? As though he's [she's] facing a tough decision or something?"

Such questions can help your child look at life through others' eyes. It takes a decision—and work—to see life as another person sees it. But the relational dividends of empathy are well worth the effort.

◇ ◇ ◇

Human relationships always help us to carry on, because they always presuppose a future.
—Albert Camus

◇ ◇ ◇

Be someone who weathers turbulence. Almost every good relationship eventually encounters a rough spot, a time when both people feel like giving up or letting go of their friendships. This is a scary phase in relationships, usually indicating that we're going beneath the surface to talk about our true feelings, our likes and dislikes, the good and the bad. It's a time of griping and whining, complaining and accusing.

We can start to teach our kids through words and actions not to give up on friendships when those friendships are less than perfect. Kids will be able to practice this trait to varying degrees as they mature. But they can start to learn the lesson from Mom and

Dad as they observe them sticking with friends when life is tough. The kids learn that if we persevere, the time of relational turbulence can lead to a deeper, more genuine, and more authentic relationship than before. Enduring through conflict is often the price we pay for a deeper connection in relationships.

DISCUSSION QUESTIONS FOR GROUP STUDY

◆ Talk about a close friend of yours. What makes this friendship so close?

◆ Friendships occasionally face bad moments. How can we keep a relationship from going solvent when the going gets tough?

◆ Think of someone you've had a relationship with for years. Why has this relationship continued so long?

◆ How can you help your children make the first steps to building friendships?

◆ When is a friendship or relationship destructive enough that it should be ended?

8

EXPECT YOUR OWN GETHSEMANE

◇ ◇ ◇

Although the world is full of suffering,
it is full also of the overcoming of it.
—Helen Keller

fter a devastating fire destroyed the main building on the campus of Olivet College in 1939, my (Les Sr.'s) father, who was the president of the college, worked with the trustees to move the school to Kankakee, Illinois, which was almost 100 miles north of its location in Georgetown, Illinois. They decided to move the college because that location offered better employment opportunities for students and had a campus with handsome buildings already in place. But the move infuriated some Georgetown residents—especially those who owned their homes. Tension increased like the volcanic pressure under the earth.

The explosion came during the wee hours of the night when the college's night watchman called Dad to the front door and then stood there passively with a nightstick in his hand while a man suddenly came out of the darkness and pummeled Dad. Barefoot and dressed only in his nightshirt, Dad had his glasses broken with the first blow, and he was unable to see. He was beaten mercilessly. The onslaught ended when I, a 15-year-old kid, came running and screaming into the living room with a revolver that neither they nor I knew was unloaded.

Mother used warm water and a washcloth to clean the blood off Dad's face. We kids were scared for our lives. No one slept the rest of that night. The night watchman reported the incident to the sheriff, who arrested the invader and put him in jail. But our neighbor (who was a faculty member) posted his bond. The next day when word of the scuffle spread through the little community, people opposing the move were delighted while my father's supporters were infuriated.

One word frees us of all the weight and pain of life: That word is "love."
—Sophocles

◇ ◇ ◇

I have watched lots of people go through their personal Gethsemane, but none ever made a bigger impression on me than what I watched my father experience. First of all, he refused to press charges against the man who had hurt him. I remember his explaining this to the family: "Going to jail or paying a fine will not change him or the feelings of the people who support him. The thing for me to do is to protect all of you the best I can, and then just keep on working toward our goal of moving Olivet College to Kankakee."

Dad never struck back at his adversary, even when the law was on his side. If he ever had an explosion of anger, I never knew about it. And, at least in my presence, he never said a derogatory word about the people who inflicted the pain.

Although this was not the last Gethsemane my father experienced, it is the one that stands out in my mind. I have often reflected upon it and his example as I faced my own difficult life experiences. And I've since come to believe that how to handle a private Gethsemane is one of the most important parts of the legacy Dad left my brother, sister, and me. It's a legacy I've tried to pass along to my boys.

You probably don't want to even consider what potential tragedy or terrible life experience might befall your children eventually, but you can be certain that somewhere in their future they will face their own private Gethsemane. Something you or they would never predict will catch them off guard. How they respond to this event will be a measure of their character. So don't neglect this important quality as you plant seeds for your children's future.

What "Expecting Your Own Gethsemane" Means

The evening was late—it was probably around 11:00 when the last candle was blown out, and the large upstairs room where Jesus ate the last meal with His disciples was clothed with total darkness. The disciples locked the door with a big iron key and returned it to the owner of the house. Turning to the narrow streets of Jerusalem, they shuffled over the cobblestones, traveling toward the East Gate.

They went down the precipitous slope from the gate to the Brook Kidron. They walked through the shallow waters and climbed up the slope on the other side. Soon they reached an old olive grove, where they stopped. Jesus said to eight of His followers, "You stay here and watch while I go farther."

He then took his three most trusted friends—Peter, James, and John—farther into the grove. But He soon stopped again. "You stay here and watch while I go over there to pray," He told them. He probably knelt next to one of the many big rocks in Palestine. Perhaps the rock gave Him a sense of privacy as He entered into the single most difficult, experience of His life.

I've seen paintings of Jesus praying in Gethsemane as though He were in quiet repose. That was not the case. He fell forward, prostrate on the ground. He was under such mental and emotional stress that His body broke out in a sweat. His forehead was coated with a mixture of blood and sweat. He groaned. He writhed like a man in great emotional pain. He moaned from the depths of His soul, "O God—with You all things are possible. If it's possible, let this cup pass from Me. But not My will, but Yours be done."

Finally arising, Jesus retraced His steps to where He had left His best friends to pray. They were asleep. He shook them awake and said plaintively, "Can't you watch with Me one hour?"

Jesus returned to His prayer corner. After an hour He returned to His disciples. For the second time they were sleeping, not watching. After the third hour of deep, soul-searching prayer, Jesus returned for the final time to find His friends still sleeping. Jesus could then see the lights from the torches of the Temple guard as they weaved their way toward Him through the olive grove. Judas was leading the pack.

By this time the disciples were fully awake, each reacting in his own way. Peter appeared angry. After all, he had let down his very best friend. Pulling a sword from its scabbard, he lifted the blade over the head of the high priest's servant. Swoosh! The blow could have been fatal, but the servant probably caught a glimpse of the upraised sword and ducked. Peter cut off his ear but was mercifully saved from becoming a murderer. Jesus scolded Peter, telling him to put away the sword. Then He attached the ear back where it belonged.

The story of Jesus' Gethsemane does not end well. No handy miracles saved Him. He was not "touched by an angel." The soldiers showed no kindness as they bound Jesus in chains like a common criminal. They led Him off to a series of kangaroo courts and eventually to the Cross to be killed.

This story is a prototype of what happens within each of us when we go through our own private Gethsemane. When that time comes—and it will—we can predict what will happen on the basis of what Jesus experienced.

To begin with, a private Gethsemane is most likely to happen in a familiar place. Judas knew exactly where he could find Jesus. Our private Gethsemane may happen in the place where we regularly worship, for example. Deep suffering occurs when a spiritual leader we counted on compromises his or her Christian standards.

Or perhaps it will happen in our homes. For the symbolic 30 pieces of silver, brothers have been known to turn against brothers. Perceived favoritism has lead to family breakdowns as divisive as the rift between Jacob and Esau, which occurred over a bowl of stew and the blessing of an aging father.

Pain is inevitable; suffering is optional.
—Unknown

We'll probably find a Judas in our Gethsemane. Judas is the one who would sell out his best friend for his own purposes. A Judas is usually someone we trust. Judas stories with modern names and settings are in newspapers almost daily. For money, government secrets are sold to the enemy by a modern Judas. Because of money, divorce settlements turn into rancorous legal battles. The Judas you experience may live with you, work with you, or attend your church. But one thing is sure—out there, somewhere, Judas is waiting to betray you in the midst of your private Gethsemane.

Finally, during your Gethsemane experience your best friends will go to sleep or follow afar off. When you need them most, it will seem as if your friends have had their telephones disconnected. Mysteriously, their E-mail won't work. They forget to return your calls. They'll disappear. And they'll plan their lives as if your situation did not exist. You will have to face your Gethsemane alone, crying out to God for mercy and relief.

Why Expecting Your Own Gethsemane Matters

A private Gethsemane is something we normally think of as happening later in life, not during childhood. And thankfully, many children are spared the lonely devastation of an unforeseen heartbreak. But far too many children do encounter their own

Gethsemane, even at an early age. Just ask the millions of children who have watched their parents divorce. Or ask the millions of kids who have survived physical and verbal abuse by adults. And don't forget the children who have suffered struggles that quietly tear at their insides because they have been singled out by classmates and tormented mercilessly, often for no reason at all.

My (Les III's) earliest Gethsemane came when I was held back in the second grade—or as my classmates said, "flunked" the second grade. My problem was reading. While other kids were turning the pages to "see Spot run," I was having a hard time just distinguishing the letters from each other.

I remember the day a specialist pulled me out of our normal reading hour, ran me though some tests, and diagnosed me with what I later learned was dyslexia. It wasn't severe. I didn't read things backward or see the words slipping off the page. But nonetheless, I had a tough time reading. So while all my friends went on to the third grade, I stayed behind to repeat the second grade.

Being held back wasn't the only thing that hurt me. I was also emotionally hurt by what happened during that school year. While other children were at recess, for example, I met with a tutor who worked with me on my reading. And twice a week after school, I met with another specialist who tried to help. With all this attention to my reading, I began feeling defective, stupid, or, as more than one classmate called me, "retarded."

As my family can attest, that's when I started throwing temper tantrums at home. My second grade tirades were serious—not your run-of-the-mill jumping up and down and screaming. These tantrums included scribbling on the wall and kicking people in the shins.

I'll never forget my dad setting me down to talk to me about my behavior. His goal wasn't to punish, but to understand. And he did. I told him how I felt about not being able to read. I told him what other kids were saying about me. He didn't swat me. He simply said, "Stay here for a moment. I want to talk to the rest of the family. I'll be right back."

Dad returned in a few minutes to tell me that our family was going out for ice cream. We piled into our station wagon and drove out of the driveway and down the street. At the corner stop sign, my older brother Roger asked me to sound out the letters on the sign. "*Ssss . . . s?*" They all clapped. "*Tttt . . . t?*" They applauded again. We drove from sign to sign as I slowly read words, and they celebrated every success.

> ### *You don't have to suffer to be a poet;*
> ### *adolescence is enough suffering for anyone.*
> ### —John Ciardi

Dyslexia. You would never know it today. My personal study is lined with floor-to-ceiling bookshelves that are packed with books I've devoured. And near my desk is a small shelf of books I've written myself. To say I eventually learned to read is true, of course, but more important, I learned to endure a difficult situation that, without my family's help, could have been an entirely different story.

How to Instill This Quality in a Child

In John 16:33, Jesus tells us that trouble in this world is inevitable. Rather than trying to keep our children's lives pain-free, we are wiser to lay a strong foundation before crisis strikes. Here are a few suggestions for doing that.

Cultivate the soil. In *Helping Kids Through Tough Times,* Doris Sanford illustrates, "The spiritual and emotional growth available for children after a death is a result of facing the pain, not avoiding it." Even if your children haven't experienced grief yet, look for opportunities to talk about death and other kinds of loss. Children's books, television shows, even current events can open doors to helpful conversation along these lines. By discussing these issues with your children, you let them know that no subject is off-limits. Then, when a loss does occur in your child's life, you'll have already begun to prepare him or her for a healthy grief process.

Listen with the third ear. I (Les III) worked with a team of school psychologists in dozens of elementary school classrooms to help students cope with the aftermath of the 1986 *Challenger* space shuttle disaster. One of our objectives was to teach how emotional jolts influence our capacity to perform effectively.

◇ ◇ ◇

*You desire to know the art of living,
my friend? It is contained in one phrase:
make use of suffering.*
—Henri F. Amiel

◇ ◇ ◇

It doesn't take a national catastrophe to influence children's ability to concentrate at school. Be sensitive to seemingly small emotional upsets that may impact their performance. You may be surprised by the magnitude of the burdens your children feel. Pay attention to nonverbal behavior (do they avoid eye contact?), and listen to the emotional tone and message camouflaged in their words. When they say they're "fine," it may mean they're depressed over a classmate's critical comments. Say, "It sounds as if you had a rough day." Without prying, this statement invites a therapeutic dialogue that can help them later focus on schoolwork. Knowing they're understood at home will help children perform well in the classroom.

Don't diminish their tough times. With the death of "Peanuts" cartoonist Charles Schulz in 2000, many commented on his ability to reflect on the sadness of real life through the experiences of his characters. In fact, analysts of Schulz's work have pointed out that every major character in Schulz's strips had an unrequited love: Charlie Brown and the little red-haired girl; Lucy and Schroeder; Linus and Miss Othmar; Snoopy and the one who dumped him at the altar. Some say that Schulz infused his strips with the depression and insecurity he had carried all his life, even from his own childhood.

Kids have more of a capacity to contemplate loss than we sometimes imagine. And they will sometimes grieve over things that seem minor to us. Think back to what it was like to be a kid. Taking second place in the science fair might not seem like a big deal to an adult—we might even think that's very good. But to a certain 8-year-old who was certain he would win first place, it may feel like the end of the world. The death of a pet is often a child's first experience with grief. Like Charles Schulz, our little ones can carry their hurts and grief into their adult years. Karen, a 32-year-old mother of two boys, remembers she was in third grade when her kitten had to be put to sleep. "I fell apart at the vet's office," she says now. "I remember my mom telling me we'd get another one, but I loved *that* kitten."

Provide an emotional safety net. During the first half of construction on the Golden Gate Bridge in San Francisco, around 20 men fell from their work to their deaths or to serious injury. Finally construction was stopped, and a giant net was built under the work area so anyone who fell would be caught. During the rest of the construction, only 4 men fell. Not only did the net make workers safer, but it also made them more confident and less likely to fall.

Parents can protect their children's dignity by making the home a safe place. Even when grades tumble, a parent's tone can make or break the spirit of a child. Parents need to respond, rather than react. Positive support, not faultfinding, increases the likelihood of better grades in the future. Berating and criticizing a student for poor grades will not make him or her work harder. Negative accusations make bad grades worse, just as they do with any other behavior. So do what you can to build an emotional safety net for your child.

Help them live with their inventory. Pastor Roger Barrier said he had never known any person intimately who was not struggling with some sort of handicap, visible or invisible. Life is filled with he-roes who won in the race of life because they would not give in to their handicap. This determination to overcome difficulties is not in the genes—it is taught.

Louis Pasteur suffered a stroke at age 46 and battled his handicap the rest of his life. Deafness did not keep Beethoven from writing some of his greatest music. United States President Franklin D. Roosevelt's influence on his country and the world was not diminished by his polio. After overcoming polio, Jackie Joyner Kersey still won gold medals.

Among the unsung heroes are those who overcame abuse, refused to be put down for their size, suffered dyslexia, had an attention deficit disorder, or lived with a weak immune system. These are the people who learned early to stop comparing themselves with everyone else. As Roger Barrier puts it, these are the individuals who "stop window shopping and live with their inventory."

We can help our kids realize that while they may have handicaps, they have so much more going right in their lives. We can teach them to count what they *can* do, not what they can't do.

Observe the good that comes from bad. When Detroit sportswriter Mitch Albom heard that his favorite college professor, Morrie Schwartz, whom he hadn't seen in 20 years, was dying of Lou Gehrig's disease, he renewed their friendship through weekly meetings. In his best-selling book *Tuesdays with Morrie,* Albom describes their visits, focusing on his old professor's wit and insights.

During one of their conversations Albom asked Schwartz why he bothered following the news since he wouldn't be around to see how things would turn out anyway. In response, Morrie offered a brilliant insight into empathy. He said that he now felt closer to suffering people than ever before. He mentioned that one night as he was watching the news on television and saw people in Bosnia running across the street, getting fired on and dying, he started to cry. "I feel their anguish as if it were my own," he said. "I don't know any of these people. But—how can I put this?—I'm almost drawn to them."

The same is true for almost anyone who is suffering, even kids. Suffering often creates a humble spirit of empathy and compassion. It often produces thankfulness.

DISCUSSION QUESTIONS FOR GROUP STUDY

◆ Did you ever see your parents go through a Gethsemane time?

◆ Can you think of a Gethsemane time in your life? How did it affect your life long-term?

◆ Talk about the different ways people respond spiritually to tough times. What happens in their walk with the Lord?

◆ How can we tell when our children are going through Gethsemane experiences?

◆ What are some practical ways you can provide an emotional safety net for your children?

MAKE YOUR FAITH YOUR OWN

◇ ◇ ◇

I respect faith, but doubt is what gets you an education.
—Wilson Mizner

reporter once asked the great theologian Karl Barth, "Sir, you have written many huge volumes about God; how do you know it is all true?" The learned German scholar is said to have responded, "My mother told me."

I (Les III) know just what he meant. I am a believer because I was raised in a believing family. I inherited my faith. I was born into a parsonage, and I was led to believe in God about the time I was old enough to eat graham crackers. Some kids sang, "Jesus loves me! this I know, / For the Bible tells me so." I might as well have sung, "Jesus loves me! this I know, / For my mother tells me so."

It's actually quite remarkable that the faith that held me so early in life is still with me. After all, I'm now about three feet taller, I have a Ph.D., I have a family of my own, and my mother lives more than 1,000 miles away. Things have changed. Still, I have the same faith—or do I?

As a child I did not weigh the evidence for accepting or rejecting various religious beliefs. In fact, I didn't even know options existed. Eventually, however, the myopic vision of my childhood was corrected. Like learning something you don't talk about in public,

I somehow discovered that not everyone believed in Jesus. In fact, my school friend Myron Goldstein hadn't even heard of Him. Still my faith hung on.

As I entered the awkward age of middle adolescence, I believed. I had a thousand doubts about myself, but my faith held strong. It survived peer pressure and a certain amount of instinctive rebellion. The memorized lines from Vacation Bible School took on meaning, and I could often quote them on cue to shield my faith from "the fiery darts of Satan." My faith was fully defended, and nothing could shake it. Well, almost nothing.

In college I learned to evaluate and question. My science professor asked me to probe and experiment. My English teacher asked me to critique Elizabethan poetry. Even my golf coach asked me to experiment with different techniques. I was encouraged to question presuppositions in almost every field. It was inevitable that I would evaluate my inherited faith and memorized answers. I remember when that evaluation began.

In the cafeteria, as a college sophomore, I suddenly saw my routine of saying the blessing at meals in a new light. It seemed perfunctory, a meaningless ritual, an unexamined but persistent—even compulsive—act. I wondered why I did it. Was it because I was genuinely thankful, or did I just want to *appear* thankful? I didn't know. Suddenly I was swimming in an ocean of doubt.

The behaviors I was taught as a child seemed superficially related to my beliefs. Prayer, going to church, reading scripture, giving to the needy, attending Bible study groups, participating in mission trips—all seemed vain. Each was like a stone in my pocket, making it more and more difficult to stay afloat.

Before being entirely submersed, I admitted my desperate doubt and found myself holding the heaviest stone yet—guilt. On top of the agony of doubt, I faced this Goliath of an emotion. I felt ashamed for doubting what seemed to be so meaningful to others. And I felt guilty for not blindly accepting their answers.

In a vulnerable moment, I remember confessing my doubt to a Sunday School teacher who quickly supplied me with a thick book of evidence and explanations. The book was meant as a lifeline, but it felt more like an anchor. My guilt grew, and I continued alone in doubt.

◇ ◇ ◇

Life is deep and simple, and what our society gives us is shallow and complicated.
—Fred Rogers

◇ ◇ ◇

It wasn't "unbelief" or stubborn resistance. This was doubt—the honest admission that in spite of all the answers, rather significant questions were still outstanding. My once articulate prayers dwindled to a single word: "Why?" This desperate question was sprayed like chemical foam on the fire of my heart. I asked the question again and again. God was silent. I took comfort in knowing that Jesus cried out the same question, but it brought me no closer to an answer.

I'm not sure how long I suffered in the darkness of doubt—perhaps six months—but somewhere in the midst of my lonely questioning, I realized I was not searching for an explanation; I was longing for a faith of my own.

What "Making Your Faith Your Own" Means

I can almost point to the spot where it happened. I was driving to Chicago's O'Hare International Airport. Dad was arriving from a business trip, and I was happy to pick him up. When I was small, Dad would almost always return from an adventure with a small gift—a model airplane from Washington, D.C., a miniature orange crate from Los Angeles, a baseball cap from Boston. The excitement of knowing Dad would pull a small package from his briefcase was enough to send me into orbit. That was long ago. On this trip I didn't expect a memento.

As I drove past the stubbled fields of February farmland, I resisted the urge to turn on the radio. I used the opportunity to spend a few minutes with the One I doubted. That's not as strange as it sounds. Most of the time I didn't really doubt God's existence—or even religious doctrines. What I did question was the Bible, God's sovereignty, the Resurrection, and miracles. But mostly I doubted my heart. I questioned the motives behind my behavior.

My prayer, like the hundreds before, continued to be filled with questions: *Why do I feel so empty? Why do You feel so distant? Sometimes I feel as if I'm a robot just going through the motions. It seems I'm more concerned with doing things right than I am with doing the right things. I want a pure heart. God, why are You so silent?*

Mingled among fond memories and softly spoken prayers, my faith began to reappear. As I drove along Interstate 55, I saw no miraculous sign. No message was written in the sky. I simply found myself anticipating Dad's arrival and humming a familiar hymn: "It Is Well with My Soul."

And it *was* well. Doubt had been quick to submerge the meaning of my faith. But in a strange paradox, my honest questioning now allowed me to grasp God's hand and be pulled from the water. And when I did, He was there—not with a lifeline or a life jacket, but as a living Lifeguard. That's when I realized I didn't need answers—I wanted a relationship. Just as I didn't need gifts upon my father's return, I didn't need answers from God. I needed to *be* with God.

Now I think I understand God's silence. It was the opportunity to view faith as more than an intellectual "amen" at the end of a religious proposition. The times I spent with Him—like driving to the airport—gave me the space to see that faith is not so much *believing* in God as it is *being* with God.

Doubt dismantled the faith of my childhood. And I thank God for doubt. It gave me faith—a faith of my own. I've come to understand what Tennyson meant when he said, "There lies more faith in honest doubt than in all your creeds." Doubt ate away my younger faith so a more mature faith could be born.

Why Making Your Faith Your Own Matters

Too often we expect continuous certainty promoted by intellectual innocence—especially from our children. We feel uneasy with, or even resent, a believer who doubts. We lose sight of the fact that faith matures because of, not in spite of, doubt. We forget that if a question is not seriously asked, a person will miss the richness and depth of the answer. In fact, the most destructive thing we can do to those passing through a period of honest uncertainty is to attempt to silence their doubts and encourage their repression. "Repressed doubts have a high rate of resurrection," John Powell explains, "and doubts that are plowed under will only grow new roots."

Faith is the "yes" of the heart, a conviction on which one stakes one's life.
—Martin Luther

Although the Bible strongly warns against unbelief, I have not found a single passage to distract us from doubt. Doubt and belief are compatible. As odd as this may sound, doubt is not a hazard to faith—rather, it may be the necessary catalyst to bring a dry and hollow faith to life.

This obviously doesn't mean the Church should aim to be a collection of doubters. It does, however, mean the Church—and parents—need not be so anxious when an honest believer confesses doubt. Parents and the Church can help young believers work through their doubts in order to construct a stronger faith.

How to Instill This Quality in a Child

While much of what we have written in the chapters of this book has been geared toward parents with children of all ages, this chapter is especially for parents with maturing kids who are entering young adulthood. Young people who are questioning, perhaps for the first time, the faith of their mothers and fathers. Here are some suggestions for helping them through this time successfully.

Take a nonjudgmental stance. Joe Nielson understands this. He taught me sociology in college. I could learn more from Prof Nielson in an hour over lunch than I could over a whole semester in some courses. He is a wise Christian teacher who helped me realize the difference between doubt and unbelief. "The unbeliever is characterized by stubborn resistance, disobedience, and rebellion," he told me. "The doubter, on the other hand, is hungry for the truth."

I can still remember the sense of relief I experienced as he said those words. He provided me with a space for honest questioning without getting clobbered with guilt. Prof Nielson understood that icy judgment only hardens an aching heart.

I am now a professor at a Christian university where I meet dozens of students each year who struggle with doubt. Their struggle is further complicated by irrational "shoulds"—guilt about what they should think, feel, or do. I often pray that these students will sense my acceptance. I am sure Dr. Nielson offered that prayer for me.

As we sense our children facing doubts in their Christian lives, we can have patience with them. Parents often tend to worry a little bit too much when older children face doubts. Sometimes we want to jump in and erase their doubts. But to develop their own faith, they must fight their own spiritual battles. We can entrust them to the Lord's hands—He loves them so much more than we do—and stand by nonjudgmentally, ready to help any time we're asked but letting them wrestle through their own battles with faith.

Don't be too quick with answers. I have learned not to answer a doubter's questions prematurely or supply him or her with a heavy book to answer for me. Many times I have seen a doubter who asks for answers but does not necessarily expect them.

Tony was like that. He sat in my office not long ago telling me how meaningful it is to question the religious life without having someone quote a line of scripture as a retort. "When someone tries to solve my questioning, it feels as if they're doing it to avoid catching my disease of doubt," Tony told me. "It makes me feel even more lonely. It would be enough to just know they care."

Tony has found a valuable key in helping doubters unlock a fresh faith. As Dr. Nielson put it, "Questions are a bridge into the presence of the One to whom they're addressed."

Sometimes our children don't need us to answer their questions, but to simply let them air their questions, to hear us agree, "That's a good question. It's one of those puzzling things about God."

Faith in God is not just believing he exists, but doing what he says because you believe he will keep his promises.
—Clayton Bell

Know that words sometimes speak as loudly as actions. According to a recent study at Purdue University, words are just as mighty as deeds when it comes to parents' passing-on of religious beliefs. The study found that children are more likely to adopt their parents' beliefs when they clearly understand what their parents believe. The researcher who conducted the study said, "We found the accuracy of a child's perception of parent's beliefs is affected by all of the things that a parent does." She said this includes taking the time to explain beliefs and encouraging the child to participate in activities the parents think support those beliefs.

No wonder Moses instructed the Israelites to talk with their children about God's commands and goodness when they got up in the morning, as they fulfilled their daily routines, and as they went to bed at night (see Deut. 6). In contrast to the cultural proverb, actions do not necessarily speak louder than words.

We can't just assume our children pick up our beliefs through being around us or going to church. To instill beliefs in kids, we need to intentionally teach our children by telling them what we feel, think, and believe about God.

Help them focus on doing the right things for the right reasons. A young priest saw a vision of God in a great cathedral. He ran to the bishop and gasping said, "I've just seen a vision of God. He's behind that pillar over there. What should we do?"

The bishop said, "Quick! Look busy!"

Do you ever feel like that with God? Sometimes we run around doing everything to try and impress God—and everybody else. The person who rates high on spiritual and mental health, however, is motivated by a genuine hunger and thirst, not outward reward, guilt, or fear.

◇ ◇ ◇

You don't have convictions unless you have been tested.
—Crawford W. Loritts Jr.

◇ ◇ ◇

In the play *Murder in the Cathedral,* T. S. Eliot wrote these lines: "The last temptation is the greatest treason; to do the right deed for the wrong reason." God does not simply want us to do what He says, but He wants us to *desire* to do what He says. He wants a pure heart. 1 Sam. 16:7 says, "Man looks at the outward appearance, but the LORD looks at the heart." Jesus said, "If you *love* me, you will obey what I command" (John 14:15, italics mine).

For a genuine faith to grow, we must learn the value of doing the right thing for the right *reasons.* And this is something we can help our children focus on. This instillment of integrity cuts down on the chance that our kids will become spiritual hypocrites—acting one way around us and another when we aren't around.

Turn the tables when you can. One day, children's television favorite Fred Rogers ("Mister Rogers") was in California and decided to visit a teenager with cerebral palsy. At first the boy was very nervous by the thought that Mister Rogers was visiting him. He was so nervous, in fact, that when Mister Rogers did visit, he got mad at himself and began hitting himself, and his mother had to take him to another room. Mister Rogers waited patiently. When the boy returned, Mister Rogers asked, "Would you do something for me?" The boy responded that he would, so Mister Rogers explained, "I would like you to pray for me. Will you pray for me?"

The boy was startled, because no one had ever asked him for something like that. The boy had always been prayed *for*. He had been the *object* of prayer, and now he was being asked to pray for someone else. Although at first he didn't know if he could do it, he said he would try, and ever since then he keeps Mister Rogers in his prayers. Formerly suicidal, he doesn't talk about wanting to die anymore, because he figures Mister Rogers is close to God, and if Mister Rogers likes him, God must like him too.

Mister Rogers was asked how he knew what to say to make the boy feel better. He responded, "I didn't ask him for his prayers for *him*; I asked for *me*. I asked him because I think that anyone who has gone through challenges like that must be very close to God. I asked him because I wanted his *intercession*."

We validate our children's faith when we ask them to lift us in prayer, to start a Bible reading program with us so that we have to be accountable to them, or to do whatever the faith-building step may be. When we ask our children to help *us* grow spiritually, not only *does* it help us spiritually, but it also grows them and our entire family together, closer to the Father.

DISCUSSION QUESTIONS FOR GROUP STUDY

◆ When did you "make your faith your own"?

◆ Have you ever faced a time of doubt in your spiritual life? How did you respond? How did you overcome the doubt?

◆ What should we do when our children are not interested in a relationship with Christ or openly rebel against a faith they've previously held to?

◆ What kinds of things keep our children from owning their faith?

◆ What are some practical things you can do to instill faith in your child?

Conclusion

In the book *The Ascent of a Leader*, Bruce McNicol and Bill Thrall tell of a woman who dreams she has wandered into a store at a shopping mall and finds Jesus behind a counter.

Jesus says, "You can have anything your heart desires."

Astounded but pleased, she asks for peace, joy, happiness, wisdom, and freedom from fear. Then she adds, "Not just for me, but for the whole earth."

Jesus smiles and says, "I think you misunderstand Me. We don't sell fruits, only seeds."

This story reminds us that when it comes to parenting our children and instilling in them the qualities for a life we want them to live, we can only plant seeds. We cannot guarantee that they will use these seeds and bear the fruit we desire. But as parents, that's all we can do—and that is enough.